BLACK VOTERS MATTERED:
A Philadelphia Story

W. WILSON GOODE, SR., D. MIN

ISBN: 978-1-54393-005-4 (print)
ISBN: 978-1-54393-006-1 (ebook)

CONTENTS

FOREWORD vi

HOW WE TOOK CITY HALL THROUGH A MOVEMENT xi

CHAPTER 1
The Northern Civil Rights Movement in Philadelphia 1

CHAPTER 2
From Protest to Politics: The Black Political Forum............. 16

CHAPTER 3
Eyes on the Prize: A Winning Campaign for Mayor............. 53

CHAPTER 4
A Mountaintop Experience... 69

CHAPTER 5
Bad Things Happen to Good People....................................... 77

CHAPTER 6
We Mastered the Process, but Not the Mission 85

CHAPTER 7
The Way Forward: Black Voting Matters................................ 91

AFTERWORD 96

ACKNOWLEDGMENTS 99

REFERENCES 101

ENDNOTES.. 102

FOREWORD

In this book, W. Wilson Goode, Sr. Philadelphia's first African American mayor, chronicles the individuals and events that played significant roles in the political empowerment of Black Philadelphia. A careful reading will validate the words of Machiavelli:

> ...It must be considered that there is nothing more difficult to carry out, nor more doubtful of success, nor more dangerous to handle, than to initiate a new order of things. For the former has enemies in all those who profit by the old order, and only lukewarm defenders in all those who profit by the new...

For those who need additional validation, read Jonathan Binzen's book <u>Richardson Dilworth: Last of the Bare Knuckled Aristocrats</u> and Ed Rendell's <u>A Nation of Wusses.</u>

Although their path was fraught with difficulties, the leaders of Philadelphia's Black political empowerment movement organized, trained and placed allies in the city's precincts, wards and neighborhoods, and cooperated with and formed alliances with other groups, institutions and leaders. They believed that change was possible if those who shared their beliefs would work together and sustain the effort. They knew that success would not come overnight, nor would that success be total. Their persistence, hard work, focus and sacrifice led to incremental and sometimes unexpected gains.

For example:

- The first Black mayoral candidate, Charles Bowser, and his Philadelphia Party lost to Frank Rizzo but succeeded in defeating Thomas Foglitetta, the Republican candidate, establishing the fact that a Black mayoral candidate could complete and possibly win.

- W. Wilson Goode, Sr. successfully registered 125,000 Philadelphia residents to vote – 100% of the eligible Black voters at the time. He also raised over one million dollars for his campaign from some of Philadelphia's most prominent business leaders.

- Goode had support from liberal and activist White voters of all ages.

- The importance of diversity in political campaigns was demonstrated when the Black Political Forum endorsed Thacher Longstreth, the White Republican candidate for mayor.

Several decades ago, a monograph "Changes and Choices" documented the changing demographics of the world population. In the last third of the 20th Century, ten percent of the population would move voluntarily (jobs, drought, and natural disasters) or forced (refugees, displaced people, war).

The Pew Research Center notes that the number of Black immigrants to the United States has more than quadrupled since 1980. As many as 3.8 million Black immigrants lived in the U.S. in 2013. Their share of the Black population is projected to rise from nine percent today to 16 % by 2060. The primary source of Black population growth in the U.S. from 2000- 2013 was a 137 percent increase in African immigrants.

Fifty percent of Black immigrants are from Caribbean nations like Jamaica and Haiti. Nine percent are from Central and South American countries. More than 80 percent live in New York and New Jersey. Many of them maintain a strong identification with their home countries. As we move forward into the future, it is clear that current models of Black political empowerment must include opportunities for these immigrant populations and an openness to all the different faces of diversity.

Philadelphia, like other cities, offers possibilities for dealing with those changes. Read Dr. Bernard Anderson in <u>Race and Community Development 2015</u> and <u>Roadmap for Growth</u> by the Greater Philadelphia Chamber of Commerce.

As we move into the next decades, it is clear that models of empowerment must include coalitions of diversity in all of its aspects. A large majority of Philadelphia residents did not vote in the 2015 mayoral election. How can voter participation be increased? How can conflicting interests in the coalition be managed? How can voters and citizens of all backgrounds be convinced that their concerns are being heard and treated with respect? More importantly, how can voters and citizens be inspired and convinced that we are all in this together, and that together we can ameliorate our problems and move forward toward a city and a nation where success is not restricted to a chosen few?

The late Dr. Manning Marable said:

> Racial minorities themselves must engage in a critical, honest dialogue about these areas of mutual concern....Like African Americans and Latinos, Asian Americans have experienced a history of discrimination and oppression....Conversely, an appraisal of racial and other realities today illustrates profound differences between minority groups....We are rapidly moving beyond the older "Black vs. White" model of race

and ethnic relations in the U.S., and African Americans must recognize the impact of this social transformation….a strategy for Black empowerment and the ability to build coalitions based on mutual self-interest with others is needed.

Factions have always existed in this city and in this highly contentious nation. The broad consensus that supposedly prevailed in earlier days is largely a nostalgic illusion. We are not and will never be a city, a nation, or a republic of virtue animated by perfect brotherhood. We are too large, too varied, too free, and too human for that. But there have always been those among us who have sought to achieve that perfection, that spirit of brotherhood, who valued compassion and who were willing to fight for the underdog, for the least favored among us. There were always those few who really believed in this country, who took its most revered documents seriously. Such persons, always in the forefront of the fight for freedom, respected the first Amendment and the Bill of Rights and had the strange belief that they applied to everyone.

To believe in America and its possibility of renewal, one must ultimately believe in individual Americans: those countless citizens, Black, White, Asian, Hispanic, rich and poor, male and female, young and old, who despite all doubts and obstacles go about their lives with courage, patience, competence and cheerful persistence, with the odd conviction that their city and their country are still experiments and must stand for something beyond survival.

For Philadelphia, that identity should be based on mutual respect, shared values, opportunity for all and a celebration of diversity.

Dr. Bernard C. Watson
Educator, administrator and foundation executive, Watson served as a teacher, counselor and principal in his hometown of Gary, Indiana; Deputy Superintendent of Schools in Philadelphia; Professor,

W. Wilson Goode, Sr.

Department Chairman and Academic Vice President of Temple University and President & CEO of the William Penn Foundation. Appointed to education commissions by Presidents Lyndon Johnson, Jimmy Carter and Bill Clinton, Watson is the recipient of the Philadelphia Award and twenty-four honorary degrees. He earned his PhD from the University of Chicago.

HOW WE TOOK CITY HALL THROUGH A MOVEMENT

The idea for this book grew out of my deep appreciation for recorded history. I've learned that unless the facts are written, people will soon forget them. So it is important to document the history of the personalities and events that led to my election in1983 as the first African American mayor of Philadelphia, to properly record and connect events so that future generations will understand and appreciate our struggle and our achievements. This book attempts to connect some of the events and personalities of the U.S social and civil rights movements with the movement in the City of Philadelphia between 1968 and 1983 that resulted in a dramatic increase in Black political empowerment. While many of the individuals involved in these events were African Americans, there were also some non-African Americans who played crucial roles in bringing about the transformation. This book will attempt to chronicle all of their roles and put them in chronological order, so that those who read this in the future will know how these events took place.

Those who read it will see that the Black pioneers who pursued public office in Philadelphia during this time were driven and purposeful, and committed to the agenda of empowering Black Philadelphians. They recognized that politics was not the end game, but rather a means to achieving genuine social change and equal justice.

It is hoped that political scientists and students of history will especially find this book useful. While the book looks at some events before 1950, the preliminary period of 1950 to 1968 was critical in bringing about the transformation that took place between 1968 and 1983. For purposes of clarity, this book will discuss the major events of my administration and the administrations of Philadelphia's subsequent mayors from 1992 to 2016, in order to illustrate the evolution of Black empowerment in the city and how these mayors came to be elected. Philadelphia has had three African American mayors.

CHAPTER 1

The Northern Civil Rights Movement in Philadelphia

PHILADELPHIA IS THE BIRTHPLACE OF THE NATION. It is the center of democracy as we know it in the United States of America. One might imagine that the quest for democratic principles burns in the hearts and souls of all Philadelphians. Two particularly significant events that took place in this city have inspired Black Philadelphians who are students of history, and demonstrate how far from equal justice the city was at one time.

The death of Octavius Catto was the first. . Octavius Valentine Catto was born on February 22, 1839 in Charleston, South Carolina to a mixed-race mother and a father who was a former slave and millwright. After he was freed, Catto's father became a minister and moved the family north to Philadelphia, where Octavius became a student at the Institute for Colored Youth (now Cheyney University). After graduation, Catto became a major player in the civil rights movement, working with the likes of Frederick Douglass to help enlist Black platoons for the Union in the Civil War. He was also an excellent baseball player who played a huge role in establishing Philadelphia's reputation in the world of Black baseball.

On October 10, 1871, Catto was on his way to vote when he was murdered by a man named Frank Kelly. Kelly was never convicted of any crime. Catto became one of the original martyrs of the Black political movement in Philadelphia.[1] His actions and protests, his unwillingness to accept a status quo that was unjust and unequal, set a precedent for the Black political movements of the next century.

The second watershed event was the Philadelphia Transportation Company (PTC) drivers' strike of 1944, when America was deep in the conflict of World War II. Philadelphia had become a major production center for war supplies. This increase in work opportunities led to an influx of population, especially among poor Black people who hailed predominantly from the South. One frequent place of employment for these people was the Philadelphia Transportation Company. However, the PTC refused to give Blacks any positions higher than that of conductor or motor-man. Retaliation against this racial discrimination climbed steadily, as the Black community reached out to the NAACP. Eventually the federal government got involved, with President Roosevelt's 1943 executive order that required every government-operated business to enforce a non-discrimination clause. This development and the increasing need for extra personnel led the PTC to decide to allow the promotion of Black employees to drivers beginning August 1, 1944. White employees attempted a sickout strike, but the federal government put an end to that within a week by threatening to enter striking employees into the military draft. The newly hired Black workers were allowed to keep their jobs.[2] This successful stand against racial discrimination foreshadowed the Civil Rights Era in Philadelphia, as well as the city's eventual election of a Black mayor.

The reform movement of 1950 produced a Home Rule Charter, which gave Philadelphia the right of self-governance. The subsequent election of the first mayor under the charter ushered in a period of progressive politics in the city. The election of Joseph S. Clark as mayor and Richardson Dilworth as district attorney planted the first seed for my election in 1983, some 33 years later.

Joseph S. Clark

Joseph Sill Clark, Jr. was born on October 21, 1901 in Philadelphia. His father was a national doubles tennis champion, and his mother's uncle had invented Tabasco sauce. He attended Harvard University and the University of Pennsylvania for law school.

After passing the bar, Clark made his first unsuccessful foray into politics in 1926. Two years later, he switched to the Democratic Party and founded the Democratic Warriors Club with Richardson Dilworth. The goal of the club was to help eradicate the political corruption that engulfed Republican-dominated Philadelphia.

After serving in World War II, Clark won the position of city controller by 100,000 votes in 1949 and used this position to investigate several corruption allegations against the Republican regime. He went on to defeat Republican mayoral candidate Daniel A. Poling in 1952, to become the first Democratic mayor of Philadelphia since 1884. Clark was the first mayor to operate under the new rules of the Home Rule Charter, and was well-known for ushering in the Clark-Dilworth era of reform in the city. After serving one term, he won a seat in the Senate and served two terms until he was defeated in 1968. He died on January 12, 1990 at the age of 88.[3]

The 1950 mayoral election was a clear break with Philadelphia's history of single party political rule, a tradition that many considered to be corrupt and non-inclusive. The election of Clark and Dilworth was a strong indication that single party rule was over. Moreover, the election of Raymond Pace Alexander and Marshall Shepherd, Sr. as part of the Clark-Dilworth team indicated that the city's new leadership wanted to be inclusive. The Progressive era would last until 1962. The establishment of the Home Rule Charter and the subsequent elections of Joseph S. Clark and Richardson Dilworth set the foundation for political empowerment for the next century.

Richardson Dilworth

Richardson K. Dilworth was born on August 29, 1898 in Pittsburgh, Pennsylvania. He attended Yale University and served in the Marine Corps in both World Wars. After unsuccessful runs at the Philadelphia mayor's office in 1947 and the state governor's office in 1950, he won the Philadelphia district attorney election in 1951 and went on to succeed Joseph S. Clark, Jr. in 1955 as the city's mayor. He and Clark were renowned for their overhaul of the Philadelphia political system. Some of Dilworth's most notable achievements in office include the reversal of the decline of Center City and his strong opposition to private school segregation. He resigned in 1962 to launch an unsuccessful second bid for governor. He was chair of the Philadelphia School Board. He died on January 23, 1974 at the age of 75. [4]

When Joseph S. Clark, Jr. was inaugurated as mayor of Philadelphia in 1951, he became the first mayor to serve under the new Home Rule Charter, which gave his office more power. New rules included the creation of a managing director position, and elected officials were banned from running for new positions without first resigning from their existing posts. Clark was the first Democrat to be elected mayor of Philadelphia since 1884. His election represented a move away from the corruption-plagued Republican regime. Clark used his new seat to help clean up the corruption in the system. He focused upon the police department and the municipal government as a whole. Clark also took this opportunity to open the concept of a career in city government to the African American population of Philadelphia – something that he claimed years later was his most important achievement as mayor.[5]

Raymond Pace Alexander

Raymond Pace Alexander was born on October 19, 1898 in Philadelphia. He was forced to work several jobs while balancing school and church after his mother died of pneumonia when he was 11. He went on to attend the University of Pennsylvania on a merit scholarship, and became the first African American to graduate from the Wharton School of Business. He got his law degree from Harvard University in 1923, and moved back to Philadelphia to begin his career.

He and his wife, Sadie Tanner Mossell Alexander, who was the first Black woman to earn a law degree from the University of Pennsylvania, went on to become powerful figures in the city. Raymond Alexander served as president of the National Bar Association from 1933 to 1935, and assisted the NAACP with high-profile cases involving the segregation of public schools in Chester County. He later served on Philadelphia City Council from 1951 to 1958, and became the first African American judge appointed to the city's Court of Common Pleas in 1959. He died on November 24, 1974. Alexander's influence on civil rights and law in Philadelphia is still felt today.[6]

In 1956 Clark became a U.S. senator and was succeeded as mayor by Richardson Dilworth. Dilworth is remembered for having continued the progressive trend in Philadelphia that was initiated by Clark. Some of the notable achievements of Dilworth's term include the revival of Center City as an economic hub, and the city's commitment to fight segregation in private schools. His term is widely considered to be a continuation of the reform movement sparked by the rebound of the Democratic Party in municipal politics, and is therefore another seed that led to the eventual political autonomy of the City of Philadelphia.

Marshall L. Shephard Sr.

Rev. Marshall L. Shepard, Sr. was born in Oxford, North Carolina, on July 10, 1899. He was educated in the public schools of Oxford, and continued his studies at Virginia Union University in Richmond, VA, graduating with a B.A. degree. He later pursued graduate studies at the Quaker Graduate Center in Wallingford, PA, and was awarded honorary doctorates by several colleges and universities. Rev. Shepard's rich background in various endeavors - including employment as a Pullman porter, steel worker and cook -both increased his skills in the area of human relations and helped to fund his college education. After prayerful consideration, the Rev. Shepard left the comparative financial security of the Abyssinian Baptist Church to become the second pastor of the Mount Olivet Tabernacle Baptist Church. His meager salary of fifteen dollars a week was hardly sufficient to support his wife, the former Lucille Owens of Sumter, SC and their family, which by then included a second son, Samuel Augustus, who is today an ordained minister. When Shepard offered the invocation at the 1936 Democratic National Convention in Philadelphia, Sen. Ellison D. (Cotton Ed) Smith of South Carolina walked out to protest the spectacle of a black man praying. When the Democrats met in Philadelphia again in 1948, Smith was dead and again Mr. Shepard gave the invocation. After winning election as the city's recorder of deeds in 1951, he became commissioner of records. He was elected to Philadelphia City Council in 1955 and was serving his third term when he died at age 67 in 1967.[7]

The Clark-Dilworth team that became the face of progressive politics in Philadelphia produced two Black elected officials. Raymond Pace Alexander became the first African American city council member, and Marshall L. Shepard, Sr. was elected as register of wills.

Robert Nelson Cornelius Nix, Sr.

Robert Nelson Cornelius Nix, Sr. (August 9, 1898 – June 22, 1987) was the first African American to represent Pennsylvania in the House of Representatives. The Robert N.C. Nix Federal Building in Philadelphia, Pennsylvania is named in his honor.

Born in Orangeburg, South Carolina, Nix attended Townsend Harris High School in New York City and graduated from Lincoln University in 1921. He received his law degree from the University of Pennsylvania and began practicing in Philadelphia. After entering private practice, Nix became active in the Democratic Party as a committeeman from the fourth ward in 1932. He became a special assistant deputy attorney general of Pennsylvania in 1934 and was a delegate to the 1956 Democratic National Convention.

In 1958, Nix defeated two opponents in a special election to fill a congressional vacancy left by Earl Chudoff in the House of Representatives. An elected official who rarely wanted or attracted widespread publicity, he supported mostly liberal legislation. He was re-elected ten times. Nix worked for the passage of landmark legislation that promoted the American Civil Rights Movement, and privately sought to prevent the House from denying Rep. Adam Clayton Powell his seat in 1967. In 1975, he introduced an amendment to the Foreign Military Sales Act, requiring the Defense Department to provide the U.S. Congress with information on the identities of agents who negotiated arms sales for American firms.[8]

While the Clark-Dilworth era was paving the way for future African American political success in the City of Philadelphia, the nation was beginning to undergo a drastic facelift in terms of civil rights. The decision handed down in the famed 1954 Supreme Court case, Brown v. Board of Education, declared that "separate educational facilities are inherently unequal"[9] , thereby clearing a path for the integration of public schools nationwide. In 1958, Robert N. C. Nix, Sr. became the first Black from Pennsylvania to be elected to the House of Representatives. Just five years later, the assassination of President John F. Kennedy in 1963 served as the impetus for much of the civil rights legislation that we continue to benefit from today, including the Civil Rights Act of 1964—which outlawed all types of discrimination based on race, gender, nationality and religion—and the Voting Rights Act of 1965, which prohibited the denial of the right to vote to any United States citizen on account of race or color. The assassination in 1968 of Martin Luther King Jr., the indisputable face of the Civil Rights Movement, prompted President Lyndon B. Johnson to pass the Fair Housing Act in 1964 ,which prohibited racial discrimination in the sale or rental of housing. King's death spurred action and reaction within the Civil Rights Movement, inspiring many Blacks to get politically involved for the first time.

Race relations were in flux during the 1960's, generating unrest within Black and White communities across the nation and especially in urban areas like Philadelphia. Tensions were particularly high during the summer of 1964 and the general unrest escalated, leading to race riots in Black neighborhoods across the nation. In August 1964, allegations of police brutality against a young Black woman on Columbia Avenue sparked two days of rioting in North Philadelphia. Later known as the Columbia Avenue riots, the uprising resulted in 774 arrests and 341 injuries, and 225 stores on Columbia Avenue were damaged or destroyed.[10] Martin Luther King's assassination on April 4, 1968 ignited another chain of riots in urban areas across the nation, amid protests and demonstrations against the Vietnam War. The death of significant political and civil rights leaders, riots and anti-war protests formed the backdrop for the 1968 U.S. presidential election.

The Republican nominee for president was former vice president Richard Nixon, who handily won the primary due to his superior campaign organization. In the general election Nixon faced off against the incumbent vice president, Hubert Humphrey, and the former governor of Alabama, George Wallace, who ran under the newly created American Independent Party. Promising to restore law and order to the nation's cities, Nixon honed in on an issue that resonated with the portion of the population that was angered by the riots of the preceding years. This tactic was part of Nixon's "southern strategy", which centered on appealing to White southerners who historically were dedicated Democrats, but could be persuaded to vote Republican due to Humphrey's support of the Civil Rights Movement. [11] Despite Nixon's efforts, Wallace ended up capturing five southern states, thanks to his racist appeals to alienated White voters, including low income White southerners and blue collar workers.

While the campaigns of Nixon and Wallace were dominated by clear strategies, Humphrey—who won the Democratic primary despite entering late—depended on the endorsement of President Lyndon B. Johnson and negative attacks on his opponents to win the election. Even with Johnson's support, Humphrey trailed Nixon in the polls throughout most of the campaign. Ultimately, Richard Nixon garnered 301 electoral votes to win the election. Hubert Humphrey won 31.3% of the popular vote, but this only translated into 191 electoral votes. George Wallace, a third party candidate, was able to win 46 electoral votes,[12] illustrating the polarization of American opinion and the power that racism and segregationist musings still had to mobilize a portion of the White southern electorate.

At the time of the 1968 Presidential election, there was no doubt that the majority of Americans were against the war in

Vietnam. Americans were able to view the casualties of war in their living rooms during the nightly news, and many families whose members had been drafted were concerned for their well-being while seeing no end to the conflict in sight. Within this national context, Blacks across the nation started to exercise the rights granted by the Voting Rights Act by voting in their local elections. Urban Blacks began to transform the political landscape by establishing political power within the Black community, something that would provide the foundation for Black politicians to get elected in years to come.

Prior to 1968, Black elected officials in Philadelphia had been hand-picked by the Democratic Party leaders of the time. Notable Black elected officials, like Raymond Pace Alexander and Edgar Campbell, served well but were chosen as candidates by the Party leadership. African Americans who ran against the wishes of the Democratic Party political machine lost, and lost badly. Nevertheless, during the 1950's and 60's, members of Philadelphia's Black community initiated independent social and political movements with the goal of increasing Black empowerment.

The first significant movement was led by the 400 Ministers, a new civil rights organization founded by Rev. Leon Sullivan and made up of the city's Black pastors. Labeled the 'consumer movement', Sullivan and the 400 Ministers aimed to leverage the power of Black consumers in Philadelphia against local employers who were charged with having discriminatory hiring practices. Through 'selective patronage campaigns', Black Philadelphians would boycott a major retailer until the company agreed to meet the 400 Ministers' demands to hire and promote Black employees.[13] The first business targeted was Tastykake Baking Company, which only employed White delivery truck drivers and had segregated locker rooms for female production workers. After the 400 Ministers announced the boycott to their respective congregations on Sunday, June 13, 1960, it took only two months to get Tastykake to agree to their demands. This was just the first victory in the Consumer Movement. Within the next three years the 400 Ministers led nine more selective patronage campaigns and convinced hundreds of businesses to comply with their demands under threat of a boycott.[14]

Leon Sullivan

Leon Howard Sullivan was born on October 16,1922 in Charleston, West Virginia. He became a Baptist minister at the age of 18, and moved to New York City in 1943 where he got his master's degree in religion from Columbia University in 1947.

In 1950, Sullivan and his wife moved to Philadelphia, where he became the pastor of Zion Baptist Church, earning himself the nickname "The Lion of Zion". In 1958, after he unsuccessfully tried to get companies to interview Black candidates for job positions, Sullivan organized a boycott campaign with the slogan "don't buy where you don't work" that proved to be extremely successful, and may have generated 1,000 jobs in the Black community over the next four years. He became a large presence in the Black community, founding organizations such as the Opportunities Industrialization Centers of America and starting initiatives such as the 10-36 Plan, which called for the Black community to consolidate in order to build a self-sufficient economic entity.

In 1971, Sullivan became the first African American on the board of a major corporation when he joined the Board of Directors of General Motors. He is the recipient of several prestigious awards, including the Presidential Medal of Freedom in 1991 and the Eleanor Roosevelt Award for Human Rights in 1999. He died on April 24, 2001.[15]

Following the success of the Consumer Movement, Leon Sullivan sought to continue to improve Philadelphia's Black community through economic empowerment. While mass protests and political activism had merit as a means of improving conditions for Black people, Sullivan believed that economic self-help was the key to incorporating Blacks into the fabric of the nation. "We Black folk must become partners at the helm of the national economy, and not continue just in menial roles, for in the final analysis Black men will be respected only in proportion to what they produce to strengthen the nation."[16] But in order for Blacks to play a more substantial role in the city's economy, Sullivan realized that the high rate of unemployment among Philadelphia's unskilled Black laborers needed to be addressed. Consequently, he devised a strategy for a job training program completely run by and for Black people that would promote self-help ideology while also providing vocational skills. This training program was housed in an abandoned North Philadelphia police station that Sullivan purchased in January, 1964 and named the Opportunities Industrialization Center (OIC). Through generous donations and gifts of equipment from local businesses, the OIC offered training in electronics, drafting, sewing and other vocations. By May of 1964, the OIC had enrolled three hundred workers in its training programs and within two years trained over 1,500 Black workers.[17]

The second major movement occurred in 1963 and was led by Cecil B. Moore, the newly-elected president of the Philadelphia chapter of the NAACP. In comparison with the Consumer movement, Moore's movement did not involve leveraging Black consumer power but instead focused on protest and confrontation. The protests were aimed against the construction of a new public junior high school in the Strawberry Mansion section of the city. While Strawberry Mansion was a predominantly Black area and the up and coming school would serve predominantly Black students, no Black construction workers were involved in building the facility. Since the construction contracts for the work had been made with the city, the lack of Black construction workers was a direct violation of the City Charter's ban on racial discrimination in municipal contracts. Moore sought to mobilize Strawberry Mansion's Black community to disrupt work on the school until the Commission on Human Relations and the city government enforced the City Charter's ban. After three weeks of picket-style protests that halted work on the construction site, an agreement was reached between the NAACP and the construction industry to hire five Black workers for the project. Plans were also made to begin a strategy to increase Black employment in other skilled trades in the city.

Cecil B. Moore

Born in West Virginia, Moore moved to Philadelphia to study law at Temple University after serving as a Marine in World War II. After earning his law degree, Moore quickly gained a reputation as a fierce and defiant lawyer who would do anything and everything in his power to help gain rights and political traction for the Black people of Philadelphia. He is best known for being the president of the Philadelphia chapter of the NAACP from 1963 to 1967. He ran unsuccessfully for Mayor in 1967. During his tenure, membership increased from around 7,000 to about 50,000. Moore was instrumental in the fight to desegregate Girard College, a boarding school designed for lower-income students from single-parent homes.[18] He was elected to City Council in the 5th Council District.

The third movement had its roots in the violent expression of discontent with the Philadelphia police department's treatment of Black citizens. On October 29, 1963, looting and violence took place in the retail district along Susquehanna Avenue, after police shot and killed Willie Philyan, a Black man with a knife. On August 28, 1964, Patrolmen Robert Wells and John Hoff responded to a domestic dispute at 22nd Street and Columbia Avenue. The commotion drew a large crowd. The crowd started to throw bricks and bottles at the policemen. Around 11:00 pm, a false rumor spread that a White police officer had killed a pregnant Black woman. Looting then spread over a large area. When all was said and done, the riots left two people dead, 33 wounded and 308 under arrest. The riots reflected the desire of Black Philadelphians to have a more equal level of participation in the city's political and criminal justice systems.

The fourth major movement took place in 1965 and was again led by prominent Black attorney Cecil B. Moore. This movement focused on desegregating Girard College, a private, all White boys' school located in North Philadelphia. The school was originally established by a large donation given to the city by Stephen Girard, who had written into his will that the city should use the funds to construct a school for "poor, orphan or fatherless White boys", who would have the added benefit of not only going to the school but living on its grandiose campus, bordered and protected from outsiders by huge cement walls.[19] The racial ban written into Girard's will was hotly contested throughout the years leading up to the desegregation campaign—including a legal suit filed by Raymond Pace Alexander in 1957[20]— but the Board of City Trusts continued to uphold the ban, which was in direct violation of the Supreme Court's Brown v. Board of Education ruling.

With knowledge of the past legal actions against the school, Moore was determined to use more aggressive tactics to force the issue of desegregation. The protest campaign officially began on May 1, 1965, with twenty picketers marching outside the Girard College walls while 800 policemen were stationed and ready to quell any potential fray. As the days turned into weeks and weeks turned into months the picketing continued, sometimes drawing members of the community as both picketers and spectators. Prominent civil rights leaders including Roy Wilkins, the national president of the NAACP, and Martin Luther King Jr. also joined the picket throughout the summer. Finally, in December, Moore stopped the picket after local officials launched yet another lawsuit to desegregate Girard College.

The suit made its way through the judicial system and was finally resolved three years later, after the Supreme Court would not uphold a lower court's ruling that maintained the segregation of the school.[21]

The fifth major movement was a high school protest that took place on November 17, 1967. The event was organized by a student-run group called the Central Coordinating Committee, led by young David P. Richardson. Around 3,500 high school students walked out of class at Germantown High School in protest, with the goal of attaining rights such as the end of the vocational tracking system; the removal of uniformed police officers from schools; and the addition of African American studies to the public school curriculum. The students were met by a large number of policemen, including newly promoted police commissioner Frank Rizzo, who was quoted as saying "Get their Black asses!"[22] Although the damage was not as significant as that from the 1964 riot, this event exemplified how Rizzo began to gain notoriety for his fierce, no holds-barred attitude. Earlier in 1967, Rizzo had been appointed to the position of police commissioner by Philadelphia mayor James H. Tate. Tate appointed Rizzo out of necessity; he had narrowly won a primary against a reformer named Alexander Hemphill, only after coercing support from the labor and city employee groups, who wanted Rizzo as police chief. The week of Rizzo's appointment, Cecil B. Moore was quoted calling him "an endorser of police brutality," and the high school protest did nothing to quiet those who felt this way about Rizzo.

The consumer movement, the Strawberry Mansion protests, the creation of the OIC, the picketing of Girard College and the student movement were all expressions of Black Philadelphians' desire for equal rights and improved socioeconomic conditions in the Black community. Together, the spirit of empowerment and change that they unleashed laid the foundation for the future of Black political power in the City of Philadelphia.

CHAPTER 2

From Protest to Politics: The Black Political Forum

———◆◆———

As the 1960's came to a close and the nation was experiencing major changes on the civil rights landscape, the local political realm in Philadelphia was going through substantial changes of its own. It became apparent to many that the successful efforts by Sullivan and Moore and the activism of David P. Richardson had fueled the inception of an independent Black political movement. The re-election of Mayor James H. J. Tate offered the perfect opportunity to kick off such a movement. Ironically, Tate was the ultimate party official. Because he had presided over the City throughout many of the movements mentioned previously, he employed Nixon's language and strategy of law and order in his campaign for re-election in 1967. Tate had assumed office after Mayor Richardson Dilworth resigned to run for governor, and he played into the Democratic machine politics that controlled the city at the time. In spite of Tate's party loyalty, the Democratic Party chairman and several other ward leaders threw their support behind former City Controller Alexander Hemphill during the primary. Receiving no support from the Democratic establishment was yet another candidate, Lenerte Roberts, a Black West Philadelphia realtor and the first Black candidate to seek a major party nomination for mayor in Philadelphia since 1923.[23]

Because Hemphill had the support of Democratic Party Chairman Joseph Smith, many expected him to win the mayoral nomination. In spite of this, Tate was backed by city employees and Philadelphia's labor unions—groups whose support garnered him 77,711 more votes than Hemphill received.[24] After Tate won the primary, he faced off against Leonard Smalls of the Consumer Party;[25]; Cecil B. Moore, who was running under the auspices of the newly created Political Freedom Rights Party[26]; and District Attorney Arlen Specter, the Republican candidate. Moore's third-party campaign was devised to illustrate the appeal of Black independent politics and to take votes away from Tate.[27] As such, his campaign consisted primarily of street corner rallies in Black neighborhoods and appeals to young Black males.[28] Smalls, the pastor of 59th Street Baptist Church, had a strong reputation in the Black community due to his work calming riots at the Eastern State Penitentiary and picketing banks downtown that refused to lend to Black people. He used his candidacy to shed light on the issues of unemployment and poverty in Philadelphia's Black community. "The current administration seems more concerned about a bigger police force and million dollar limited emergencies than eradicating the poverty of our people," stated Smalls in an interview with the *Philadelphia Tribune*.[29]

Leonard Smalls

Leonard Smalls was born in 1930 in White Plains, New York, where he observed the racial inequality of the time. Smalls went to college at Virginia Union University. While he was there, he participated in various pickets and protests. After a stint in the army, he moved to Philadelphia to work at a ministry near the 7th Avenue Subway.

While working at the ministry, Smalls was asked by an acquaintance to help calm down riots at the Eastern State Penitentiary. The penitentiary had never had a Black chaplain, but Smalls did everything in his power to get that changed, and he became the first Black chaplain at the penitentiary in 1958. Smalls continued to gain respect in Philadelphia, and soon became involved in the fight against the unfair business practices being used to manipulate the poor people of the city. Targeting ridiculous interest rates and bogus loans, Smalls linked up with the Consumer Party, a political party that emphasized bringing an end to these issues. In 1967 he decided to run for Mayor. Smalls was a distinguished Pastor in Philadelphia, serving Bethlehem Baptist Church in Penlynn, Pennsylvania and the 59th Street Baptist Church in Philadelphia. [30]

Specter's campaign focused on the party politics of the Democratic machine. With a slogan of "We need *these* guys to watch *those* guys," Specter argued that the Republican minority was needed to curb the abuses of the Democratic majority.[31] Some voters were open to voting for Specter, who was well-known in Philadelphia as the former district attorney, in spite of the fact that he had changed parties and was running as the Republican candidate. Moreover, there were a number of voters who felt that Tate was a know-nothing who had done little for the city while in office, and therefore needed to be replaced.

Even with two well-known Black candidates and the popular district attorney Specter in the race, Tate's defeat was not a sure thing. Tate had the backing of city employees and labor unions. In addition, he appointed Charles Bowser as deputy mayor in June 1967, making Bowser the first Black to hold the position in the city and garnering some support from Philadelphia's Black community.[32] As former director of the Philadelphia Anti-Poverty Action Committee (PAAC), Bowser was responsible for managing an organization that met the federal requisites for an anti-poverty program, while also directing funds from the Office of Economic Opportunity to areas in need in Philadelphia. He was well-known and respected not only in the city's Black community, but in Washington, D.C. as well. The Chair of the Anti-Poverty Program was Samuel London Evans, a shrewd community and political operator. In essence, Bowser's appointment was a strategic move by Tate to woo the Black vote from Moore and Smalls, and in the end it was the Black vote that gave Tate his re-election victory.

Samuel L. Evans

Samuel L. Evans, the patriarch of Philadelphia's African American leaders, a toughened veteran on the civil-rights struggle, and a longtime power broker in city politics, died on June 3, 2008 at the age of 105, at the St. Agnes Continuing Care Center in South Philadelphia.

Mr. Evans, who was born a year before the Wright brothers' first successful airplane flight and during the presidency of Theodore Roosevelt, continued to do his daily toe-touches and knee bends until his health began to decline. He was well over 6 feet tall and walked ramrod straight.

Through the American Foundation for Negro Affairs (AFNA), which he founded in 1968, Mr. Evans provided a mentoring program that helped hundreds of youths go on to professional careers.

From at least 1963, when he organized Philadelphia's 43,000-member contingent to the Rev. Dr. Martin Luther King Jr.'s historic march on Washington, Mr. Evans was a force in Democratic city politics.

By the early 1940s, Mr. Evans was being referred to as a lieutenant of John B. Kelly, the brickwork contractor who had become a city Democratic chairman. His first government job was as Philadelphia coordinator for Black activities in the physical fitness program of the U.S. Office of Civilian Defense.[33]

While Moore and Smalls won 15,336 votes between them, Tate won every Black ward in the city, which gave him 78,629 votes and effectively negated the Black votes that Moore and Smalls had won. Meanwhile, Arlen Specter won the predominantly White wards in northeast and South Philadelphia. In the end, Tate received 42,590 more votes than Specter in Black wards, and it was this majority that gave him his overall margin of victory.[34] What made Tate's strong showing so significant was that, other than the strategic appointment of Charles Bowser as deputy mayor a few months before the general election, Tate had done nothing special to attract the Black vote. In the past, Tate had taken the Black vote for granted, just as the Black vote had historically been taken for granted by Philadelphia's Democratic machine, but this time Tate recognized that his political future depended on a strong Black turnout, and Bowser's appointment enhanced his chances. Therefore, 1967 was a landmark year for Black politics in the City of Philadelphia. While the two Black candidates' motives weren't entirely similar - Moore ran to loosen the grip of the Democratic Party on Black politicians, and Smalls ran with the Consumer Party to fight against economic injustice for all races - the significance of getting two candidates on the ballot was important to the movement.

This election might have been completely different had the Black Political Forum, which was established a year later, already been in existence when it took place. Much more will be said about the BPF, which was organized in 1968 to help Black Independent political candidates. As John F. White, Jr. explained in reference to Moore's campaign, "Cecil did not have the benefit of a BPF in 1967. He didn't have the tentacles that could reach out into the city in different parts where Black people were living." [35] Still, setting precedent is everything in politics, and Smalls and Moore doubled their impact by running at the same time.

After the 1967 mayoral election in Philadelphia, many prominent Black leaders realized that the Black vote was something to be coveted and not disregarded by local politicians. As Carl Stokes in Cleveland, Ohio and Richard Hatcher in Gary, Indiana won their elections to become the first Black mayors of their respective cities in 1968, the desire of Philadelphia's Black leaders to establish independent Black political power in the city only grew.

Prior to 1968, there were a few Black representatives in Philadelphia's City Council and the Pennsylvania State legislature, handpicked by the Philadelphia Democratic machine and with little interest in, or ability to bring about substantive change for their communities. One of these representatives was Raymond Pace Alexander. Alexander, born in 1898, grew up in Philadelphia and was the first Black graduate of the University of Pennsylvania's Wharton School of Business. After getting his J.D. at Harvard Law School in 1923, Alexander returned to Philadelphia to found the city's premier Black law firm. Before he was elected to City Council, Alexander's career was defined by a series of legal successes in the field of civil rights. As a legal representative for the NAACP, Alexander prevented the establishment of racially segregated schools in Chester County in two separate cases in 1939. His brief from the case was used by Supreme Court Justice

Thurgood Marshall in the famous case Brown v. Board of Education, which led to the nationwide desegregation of schools in 1954.[36]

With his election to City Council in 1951, Alexander became the first Black councilman to represent North Philadelphia as a member of the Democratic Party. Representing a district that included Girard College, Alexander helped to develop the legal framework that put an end to the exclusion of Black students from that institution. He served on the City Council until 1958, when Governor George Leader appointed him to be a judge on the Court of Common Pleas, the first Black person to hold that title. Alexander would continue to serve on the bench until his death in 1974. It must be mentioned that Marshall Shepherd was elected register of deeds the same year that Alexander was elected to Council. Marshall L. Shepherd, Sr. later became a City Council member-at-large and was pastor of the 3,000 member Mt. Olivet Tabernacle Baptist Church. He was a civil rights leader and a powerful force in the city during his time.

While his political and legal achievements were nothing to scoff at, Alexander was unfortunately held back by the time in which he lived. Like the other Black representatives backed by the Democratic Party in Philadelphia before 1968, Alexander's political career was subordinate to the goals of the Party. However, he played an integral role in blazing the trail that would enable members of the Black community to overcome the Democratic Party political machine.

Cecil B. Moore was another prominent Black leader of the time. Born in West Virginia, Moore moved to Philadelphia to study law at Temple University after serving as a Marine in World War II. After earning his law degree, Moore quickly gained a reputation as a fierce and defiant lawyer who would do anything and everything in his power to help the Black people of Philadelphia. He was instrumental in organizing the protests that ended the exclusion of Black students from Girard College, He was also renowned for taking on hundreds of pro-bono clients, many of whom elected to spend months in jail in order to wait for their turn to employ Moore as their defense attorney. Moore is best known for being the president of the Philadelphia chapter of the NAACP from 1963 to 1967. In 1967, he decided to run for mayor without the support of the Democratic Party.[37] While he failed to get enough properly formatted signatures to officially get on the ballot, he set a precedent by being the first Black politician to run without the backing of the Democratic Party – the first building block in the rise of Philadelphia's Black community to independent political sovereignty. This impetus would begin to skyrocket a year later with the founding of the Black Political Forum.

Despite the fact that these early Black leaders were working toward the same goal, they didn't always see eye to eye. Moore was well- known for his defiant personality and he was not one for compromise or partnership; nor was he a fan of Alexander's approach. Moore's reluctance to back down showed when he demanded that the newly elected Mayor Tate appoint three African Americans to high positions.[38] While Tate didn't fully honor this request, he did appoint Charles Bowser to the position of deputy mayor, the highest position an African American had ever held to that point in Philadelphia. Bowser would eventually go on to run for mayor himself in 1975 and 1979, and his appointment as deputy mayor was another expansion of Black political influence that helped to push boundaries in the city of Philadelphia. Cecil B. Moore would go on to be elected to City Council in the 5th District.

While the Democratic Party was still strong and in control in Philadelphia in 1967, political figures like Raymond Pace Alexander and Cecil B. Moore contributed to the steady development of Black political sovereignty, through legal battles, demonstrations, appointments of Blacks to higher positions, and breaks with Democratic Party tradition. All of these factors would culminate in the creation of the Black Political Forum.

In 1968, Hardy Williams, a prominent Black attorney and community activist, met with church leader John F. White Sr. to discuss the state of politics in the city. I was also at that meeting in the role of community leader. A year earlier, Richard Gordon Hatcher had been elected mayor of Gary, Indiana and Carl Stokes had been elected mayor of Cleveland, Ohio, making them the first Black mayors of large U.S. cities. The grassroots victories of Stokes and Hatcher gave us hope that significant change could be won by Philadelphia's Black community as well. But first, the Black vote needed to be unhinged from Philadelphia's Democratic machine. During our meeting, Williams, White and I agreed to form an organization that we hoped would give an independent political voice to African Americans in Philadelphia, and break the Democratic Party's stranglehold on political leadership in the Black community. We named this organization the Black Political Forum (BPF).

The organization was founded on three core beliefs: Black people must control the institutions that control their lives; political power is the major force for gaining that control; and the Black community must be liberated from political enslavement as soon as possible. This last belief was aimed to remedy the stranglehold that the Democratic Party had on the Black community and Black candidates. Historically, the Democratic Party handpicked Black candidates that it would support, as long as they were loyal to the Party's agenda, which meant that at times they had to choose between Party loyalty and being loyal to their constituents. . The lack of responsiveness of their Black elected officials had led most Black Philadelphians to become apathetic about local electoral politics in general. On February 22, 1969, Austin Norris, a journalist for the *Philadelphia Tribune*, penned an article on the conundrum of Black politics in the city:

For Negroes, there is a substantially low percentage of government officials and politicians representing their important interests. Most of these important Negro officials have been selected by white leadership, which substantially reduces their independence and courage in representing us. But even more important, they stand almost alone without the support of intelligent Negroes pressing and demanding needed improvements and remedies for our problems. Neither white nor Negro politicians feel the pressure of intelligent Negroes through church or civic organizations, for there is very little being applied…The fact that there is very little grass-roots interest in the solution of their problems through the ballot box has resulted in Philadelphia Negroes being mere wards of the City, with very little voice in directing their own destiny, or that of our city, although they are the largest racial or ethnic group in Philadelphia.[39]

J. Austin Norris

J. Austin Norris was born in 1893. He came to be known in Philadelphia as a prominent and politically influential African American lawyer. He was well-known for his work in the Seventh Ward, and he also wrote editorials in several news-papers and served on the Board of Revision of Taxes. In 1955, he began to work for the first Black law firm in Philadelphia, Norris, Schmidt, Green, Norris, and Higginbotham. The firm went on to produce a large number of legal and federal officials including: A. Leon Higginbotham, federal judge, Clifford Scott Green, federal judge, Herbert J. Hutton, federal judge, Harvey Schmidt, common pleas, and Hardy Williams, state senator. Norris died in 1976.[40]

Agreeing with Norris' sentiments, White and I planned a two-pronged approach for the BPF. First, the organization would make sure that the public (especially the Black community) knew how Black candidates were presently being selected to run for office. Second, the organization would strategically support Black candidates who were running independently of the Democratic Party.

Williams, White and I all brought different things to the creation of the Black Political Forum. Hardy Williams was a visionary innovator and bold courageous thinker; without him, the movement would not have begun when it did. John F. White, Sr. was the leader who held the organization together for eight critical start-up years, when his leadership skills propelled the BPF. I was the tactician, strategist and researcher, focused on developing winning campaign models. While others also played significant roles in the development of the BPF, at the end of the day, it was the three of us whose actions led to the early successes of the movement.

Thirty people from across Philadelphia attended the first meeting of the Black Political Forum. While the agreement to form the organization was not unanimous, an overwhelming majority agreed that there was a need for such an entity. The group agreed on the name Black Political Forum (BPF) and the following officers were elected: John F. White Sr., president; Dr. George French, vice president; Salina Gary, secretary. I was elected as strategist and chairman of the Political Action Committee.

John F. White Sr.

John Felix White was born in Berlin, Maryland on June 9, 1924. Receiving a bachelor's of science degree from Bowie State College in 1944, White went on to Cedar Crest College where he received a certificate of Christian education.

White served as deacon at Mount Carmel Baptist Church in West Philadelphia, where he became a well-known organizer and strategist. In 1968, he and others created the Black Political Forum (BPF) which brought Black leaders together to work on ways to maximize the influence of the Black community in Philadelphia politics. The BPF eventually became a leading political organization for Independent Black politics in the city, responsible for the election of prominent Black officials such as Hardy Williams, David P. Richardson, John F. White Jr. and William H. Gray III. [41]

The BPF was comprised of committed men and women who were actively striving to bring political education to the Black community and encourage Blacks to develop independent voting habits. To pursue its mission the BPF planned retreats; formed political education institutes, including an hour-long weekly radio program on WHAT with host Mary Mason; arranged poll watcher training; organized strategy sessions; and provided support for candidates who were running independently of the major parties. Mary Mason was a prominent Black radio personality who had great influence in Philadelphia. She was a talk show host who sought to mold public opinion through her show. Her influence was critical during the formative years of the Black Political Forum, and she would continue to be a great influence in Philadelphia politics and social action throughout the 1970s and 80s.

At the time, John F. White Jr. was only a child sitting in the background listening to the group's discussions. He recalled:

> The groundwork was laid for....an agenda to address the needs and concerns of the African American community. The BPF had influence because of Black radio. You had the emergence of Black talk radio with Mary Mason and Georgie Woods. These stations had primarily been [about] hip-hop and rock music, but all of a sudden Mary Mason took phone calls when she was doing gospel in the morning. I don't remember what the issue was, but she had someone from the Forum call in to the radio station and....I had never heard that before. I had never heard of someone calling in other than to make a request for a song. And they were willing to take a phone call about an issue affecting the Black community, and that took off.[42]

As the result of its connection with Mary Mason's show, the BPF was eventually able to create its own program, which aired on

Sunday afternoons. Says White, Jr, "You'd be surprised....how many people listened after [the show was on at] the same time every week. It generated a real following and people began to talk about it. I think that had a tremendous impact on sparking the interest of people who wanted to make a difference."[43]

In 1969, the BPF backed Joseph Coleman, a chemist running for city controller, and Ben Johnson, a renowned defense attorney who was running for the Pennsylvania Senate in the 7th District. Both candidates were unsuccessful, but this did not discourage the BPF, which was really aiming for a state House seat. Eleven years later, Joseph Coleman would become the first African American president of Philadelphia City Council in 1980.

In 1968, Hardy P. Williams ran for Democratic committee leader of the 3rd ward. Committee leaders were an important cog in the Democratic machine, and the Black Political Forum sought to use these positions to undercut the machine's hold on the Black community. Williams ran against community leader Dorothy Brennan and won. The *Philadelphia Tribune* reported, "(Hardy) Williams' victory demonstrated the vulnerability of the machine in Black neighborhoods, and set the stage for the BPF campaigns for elected office."[44] In a recent interview, Anthony Williams spoke of his father:

"So that would have been 1968 or '67, probably '68. He came to me and said....'I want to get your opinion about something. I was offered a job as Judge. I don't think I'm going to take it. What do you think?' As any 8 or 9 year old would say, [I said] 'Do what you want to do,'[which] wasn't the answer my mother wanted. So that Monday we got the call and [my father had been] fired. Austin Norris said, "He's ruining his career, he'll never work in Philadelphia again." My dad wasn't home, so I didn't know what he was crying about."[45]

Austin Norris, the founder of one of Philadelphia's Black law firms, had arranged for Anthony Hardy Williams' father to be appointed Judge, which at that time would have been a real plum position. However, Hardy Williams knew that becoming a Judge would have taken him out of political engagement forever, and he saw the offer of a judgeship as a way to buy him off. Norris, the influential power broker, felt that Williams' refusal to take the judgeship was a slap at him, so he fired Williams. Putting principle above political position cost Hardy Williams his job, but it strengthened him in the political movement. Had Williams taken the judgeship, there probably would not have been a Black Political Forum.

In 1970, the Black Political Forum held its first banquet, with Mayor Richard Hatcher of Gary, Indiana – the first Black mayor of a large city -- as its keynote speaker. The banquet was attended by more than 1,000 people, and it established the BPF as a major player in Black politics in Philadelphia. In May, the BPF backed Hardy Williams in his run for state representative of West Philadelphia's 191st legislative district, against Paul Lawson who was backed by the Democratic machine. The BPF assigned me, as its chief political strategist, to serve as Williams' co-campaign manager alongside Paul Vance, an up and coming superstar in education who would later become superintendent of schools in Montgomery County, Maryland and Washington, D.C. Members of the BPF and Williams' campaign staff visited Gary, Indiana and Cleveland, Ohio in an effort to learn more about Hatcher's and Stokes' respective campaign strategies and operations. Many of the lessons learned from Hatcher and Stokes were applied to Williams' campaign. Williams focused his campaign on youth issues, including education and gang violence. He organized youth protests related to these issues and encouraged other Black elected officials to join him.

<u>Hardy Williams</u>

A Philadelphia native, Hardy Williams was born on April 14, 1931. He attended West Philadelphia High School and then went onto Cheyney University. Williams later transferred to Pennsylvania State University where he became the first Black basketball player in the school's history. As team captain, he led the school to its first tournament championship in 32 years.

After graduation, Williams attended the University of Pennsylvania Law School where he was elected to the honor society and earned his LLD. Shortly thereafter, he was appointed to the City Solicitor's office. He resigned from this office in 1965 to run for City Council as an independent Democratic candidate.

In 1970, Williams was elected to the Pennsylvania State Legislature and just two years later ran for mayor of Philadelphia. Despite his loss, Williams was the first Black mayoral candidate whose candidacy garnered widespread support, and his campaign laid the groundwork for future Black mayoral candidates in the city.[46]

Recalled White, Jr.:

I remember we marched from 52nd and Chestnut all the way down to City Hall and chanted: 'I don't want to die; I want to live,' and I'll tell you who was there—Hardy Williams and other members of the Forum [including] Dave Richardson, John F. White, Sr. and myself," "You couldn't find one other Black elected official who was willing to get in the street and protest that there was nothing being done to end…. gang violence. Not one.

They were in office, but not one came; almost like it was beneath them. Worse than that...was their silence.[47]

Williams challenged whether Paul M. Lawson was a resident of the district, and more importantly, whether he ever spent any time there. Despite these questions, Lawson was a formidable opponent for Williams, due to his Party backing and his reputation as the protégé of Isadore Shrager, the leader of the 60th ward. In 1970 Shrager, who was White, had managed to maintain control over a ward that was 95 percent Black. Consequently, he held a lot of political sway and was the personification of everything the BPF was fighting to overcome in regard to the Democratic machine. A victory over Lawson would be the breakthrough the Forum was seeking. The Williams campaign remained diligent and felt that it could win by knocking on every door and duplicating the presence of the Party and the union at each polling place on Election Day. Campaign volunteers, many as young as high school students, knocked on doors every evening and weekend. This strategy proved to be effective and Williams defeated Lawson handily, with nearly 60 percent of the vote. The victory made Williams the first African American to be elected independently to represent the Democratic Party in the 285-year history of Philadelphia.

Williams' win over Lawson in the primary signaled to both the Black community and the Democratic Party that the Black vote could no longer be taken for granted. Never before had so many low and middle income Blacks registered and turned out for an election. Moreover, Williams' election cemented the effectiveness of the BPF's mobilization and campaign training strategies. While Lawson's campaign had experience and money, generally the most important factors in an election, Williams' campaign had demographic advantages, a thirst for victory, and a more dedicated volunteer corps. Williams was a candidate who had been trained and supported by the BPF, and when facing the longstanding, well-funded and well organized Democratic machine, he had won.

"Hardy was the 'Pied Piper' for guys like [David P.] Richardson and [me]," recalled John F. White Jr. "He was fiery and committed to the community, not quite anti-establishment, but challenging to the establishment."[48] Ultimately, William's presence in the state House was a major step toward the Black Political Forum's goal of electing leaders who would be policy makers, not just symbolic place-holders.

The following year, Hardy Williams attempted to take substantive representation a step further by entering the Democratic primary for mayor in 1971. He ran against Congressman William (Bill) Green; City Councilman David Cohen; and Frank Rizzo. Even though Williams had a history-making position as state representative, he and the BPF sought to ensure that a Black candidate could be a viable candidate for mayor in Philadelphia, while also signaling that Blacks would now be seeking the top political position in the city. Understanding that his campaign was yet another step on the road to establish Black political power in Philadelphia, Williams told me, "I'm not going to be the first African American mayor of the city, but you will."[49] Little did Williams know that in just 12 years his prophecy would come true.

Hardy Williams' campaign for mayor—officially announced at the BPF's Black Political Convention in February 1971-- focused on registering Black voters and mobilizing the Black vote. In a January speech to the Philadelphia Chapter of Americans for Democratic Action, Williams spoke about the connection between his presence in the race and mobilizing the Black vote in Philadelphia. "A Black candidate would motivate registration, a larger turnout in the elections [and] the hope that the political system offers a method of change and would…. involve the noninvolved."[50] Williams and the BPF realized that only through a strong mobilization effort would they ever have a chance of beating the favorite in the race, Frank Rizzo.

I first met Frank Rizzo in August of 1970, when he was already "acting mayor" under Mayor James H. J. Tate's plan to get Rizzo elected. At the time, I was president of the Paschall Betterment League and was blocking traffic on Woodland Avenue at Island Road during rush hour each day to convince the city to put a Recreation Center at that location, rather than a halfway house for prisoners. After a month of stopping traffic, I got a call from Fred Corleto, the city's managing director, who said that Rizzo wanted to meet with me in Corleto's office. It was a very brief meeting. Rizzo said, "Stop demonstrating; you will get what you want after I am elected officially" – and he kept his word.

Due to his tumultuous interactions with Philadelphia's Black citizens, Rizzo was widely disliked by Blacks but very popular in Philadelphia's blue collar neighborhoods. He benefitted from the endorsement of the Democratic City Committee, and had widespread name recognition from his former position as police commissioner. Rizzo's campaign attacked the liberal elites for not doing enough to stop Black militant groups in Philadelphia during the protests and riots of the previous years, and despite the racism embedded in his campaign, he maintained support from seven of the sixteen Black ward leaders of the Democratic Party.[51] In stark contrast to Rizzo were his opponents, Bill Green and David Cohen. Green was the son of Philadelphia's machine boss, but surprisingly, his campaign focused on liberal political reforms. Meanwhile, Cohen's platform focused on police reform, protecting the rights of protesters, supporting the Black community's desire to have more control over public institutions, and most importantly, defeating Frank Rizzo.

The contrast between the three White candidates led some to believe that Williams—as the sole Black candidate—could benefit from a split in the White vote. By splitting the White vote, mobilizing Black voters and attracting enough White liberals to his camp, Williams could potentially win the primary. Unfortunately, Williams' campaign suffered from inadequate funding and a lack of real support beyond the Black community. There was also a rumor that the Rizzo campaign was secretly funding Williams in an effort to split the White vote—a tactic that may have drawn some White liberals away from Williams' campaign.[52]

Rizzo's biggest opponent became Bill Green, who had earned the support of Americans for Democratic Action and a strong endorsement from David Cohen. Cohen had dropped out of the race two weeks before the election. Despite Green's popularity and strong endorsements, Hardy Williams stayed in the race, insisting that the Black candidate shouldn't be the one to drop out. In the end, Rizzo defeated Green by 48,000 votes and Williams by 130,000. What was noteworthy about this election was that Hardy Williams received 50,000 votes. Furthermore, Green earned more votes in Black wards than Williams did—illustrating that Black voters were voting for the most viable candidate as opposed to just voting based upon race. Arguably, had Williams dropped out of the contest, Green would have had enough votes from Black voters and White liberals to defeat Rizzo in the primary election.[53] But, it should be pointed out that the presence of Williams in the race inspired increased Black voter registration.

Williams' election results were striking - this was the first time that a Black mayoral candidate in Philadelphia had earned 50,000 votes. Such a large number of votes made Williams the first credible Black mayoral candidate in the history of Philadelphia politics. What's more, Williams' determination to expand independent Black political power in the city continued even after his mayoral defeat. He went on to organize the Pennsylvania Legislative Black caucus, which was intended to harness the power of Black elected officials to act and vote independently when it came to matters affecting African Americans across the commonwealth. Williams also helped to further the campaigns of other independent Black Democrats throughout the city.

Also running in the 1971 primary election for City Council member-at-large was Georgie Woods, a nationally known Black radio personality and talk show host. Woods ran as a Republican and on election night was declared the winner, only to have this result invalidated by a recount. There was great suspicion in the Black community that the election had been stolen. Many felt the Republican Party did not want Woods to win because it had its eyes set on his opponent, Tom Foglietta, to run for mayor in 1975. Interestingly enough, Foglietta did resign from Council and ran for mayor in 1975, but came in third behind Bowser who was a third party candidate.

In the 1971 November general election, Frank Rizzo faced Republican Thacher Longstreth - city councilman, president of the Chamber of Commerce and former president of the Philadelphia Urban league. Longstreth entered the general election planning to use the Black vote to his advantage. Claiming that he had been more involved with the Black community than any other White man in Philadelphia, Longstreth planned to attract Black voters by relying on his heavy involvement with groups like the United Negro College Fund, the Urban League, the Urban Coalition and the NAACP. But there was a lot of skepticism as to whether his involvement with these groups would be enough to convince Black voters to vote across party lines. In opposition to the desires of the Black community, Longstreth had opposed a $2 per hour raise for hotel employees, and supported the Crosstown Expressway and the Market Street East Project. Moreover, the groups with which Longstreth was involved were predominantly made up of middle-class Blacks, thereby leaving the broad base of the low income Black community unimpressed.[54] This skepticism was soon put to rest after Longstreth earned the endorsement of the Black Political Forum.

Longstreth had spoken to the BPF during its Second Annual Mid-Summer Conference in August 1971. Frank Rizzo was also invited to this conference but declined, signaling an apparent lack of interest in Black issues and in attracting Black votes.[55] During the conference Longstreth reiterated his connections with the Black community, especially his support of Black businesses in Philadelphia. The BPF quickly realized that supporting Longstreth would reflect the newfound political independence of Black voters from the Democratic Party. Longstreth also knew that the BPF's endorsement would help him secure the Black voting base that he needed to defeat Rizzo. Along with Longstreth, the BPF endorsed three other Republican candidates, including Dr. Ethel Allen, an osteopathic physician running for the North Philadelphia 5th District council seat held by Thomas McIntosh, an avid Rizzo supporter. In an effort to support Dr. Allen's candidacy, women involved in the BPF formed a new organization, the Black Women's Political Alliance.

Ethel D. Allen

Ethel D. Allen, D.O. (May 8, 1929 – December 16, 1981) was an African American Republican politician and physician who served in the Pennsylvania state cabinet as Secretary of the Commonwealth.

Allen was born in Philadelphia, Pennsylvania. She studied at West Virginia State College, where she majored in chemistry and biology with a minor in mathematics, and went on to earn her Doctor of Osteopathy from the Philadelphia College of Osteopathic Medicine in 1963.

As a self-described "ghetto practitioner," Allen worked in difficult and often dangerous circumstances in some of Philadelphia's poorest neighborhoods. At one point, she was lured to a false house call and found herself the target of a robbery. Four men had surrounded her, hoping to get drugs from her medical bag, but she escaped safely after wielding her gun and sending the would-be robbers running.

Allen decided that the best way for her to combat the crime she saw as a practicing physician was to become more involved in politics. In 1971, she ran for Philadelphia City Council. That year, buoyed by a series of strong debate performances, she unseated incumbent Democratic Councilman Thomas McIntosh in the 5th District. With her election, she became the first African American woman to serve on City Council. In 1975, Allen decided to seek re-election to Council, but this time ran for one of Council's at-large seats. She won one of the two seats allotted for the minority Republican Party, taking over the seat vacated by Tom Foglietta, who was the party's nominee for Mayor in that year's election.56She later served as Secretary of the Commonwealth of Pennsylvania.

As the general election drew closer, Longstreth also won the support of the *Philadelphia Tribune* and many influential Black leaders, including Rev. Leon Sullivan; Cecil B. Moore; Reverend Marshall Lorenzo Sheppard, Sr., pastor of Mt. Olivet Baptist Church; Phillip Savage, Tri-State NAACP Director; and Maude Roberts, business-woman and civic leader. Announcing their support at an October press conference in Progress Plaza, these leaders cited Rizzo's avid racism and disregard for the Black community as their rationale for supporting Longstreth. Said Moore, "This is the only city in the world where a man is running for mayor who is more concerned about whipping Black heads than about solving the problems of education, gang wars and drugs. We're endorsing Thacher Longstreth because we want a man who's going to be mayor of all the people, not just certain people."57

The support Longstreth received from the BPF and influential Black leaders resulted in a large amount of ticket splitting among Black voters. Through voter registration drives and a citywide telephone chain with the message, "Split or Vote Straight Republican for Longstreth", Longstreth won nearly all of the city's Black wards.58 Despite Longstreth's showing in the Black community, Rizzo maintained his White voter base, which enabled him to win the election.

Yet, through the hard work of the BPF and the Black Women's Political Alliance, Dr. Ethel Allen defeated Thomas McIntosh by 4,000 votes, making her the first Black woman to win a City Council seat in Philadelphia. Stating that her election would "give a shot in the arm to independent Blacks [and] confidence to the young Black people of Philadelphia," Dr. Allen thanked the supporters of Hardy Williams, the Black Political Forum, the Black Women's Political Alliance, and the coalition of Democrats, Republicans and Independent voters that led to her victory.[59]

The defeat of Thomas McIntosh by Dr. Ethel Allen was a significant achievement. Many different interests converged to bring about this victory. There was a strong anti-Rizzo vote in the 5th Council District. The Black Political Forum had a strong desire to remove Tom McIntosh from office because of his uncompromising allegiance to the Democratic Party at the expense of those who lived and voted in the 5th District. It was also helpful that Hardy Williams was running for mayor, and that the 5th Council District gave Williams his biggest support.

As Hardy Williams' campaign manager and the chief political strategist for the BPF, I was able to pull together all the resources of these various interests to increase the likelihood of a win for Dr. Ethel Allen. This was a difficult challenge. The 5th District was 95% Democratic, so getting people to split their votes was a unique undertaking. Many often pulled the Democratic lever, but getting them to vote for a Republican took some additional organizing. But it showed that the Black electorate had an independent mindset when it mattered.

Another noteworthy win for the BPF in 1971 was the election of Judge Robert N.C. Nix, Jr. to the Pennsylvania Supreme Court. The son of Philadelphia's first Black congressman—Robert N. C. Nix, Sr., who was elected in 1958—Nix, Jr. decided at the age of 12 that he would pursue a career in law. After attending Villanova University and graduating from the University of Pennsylvania's law school in

1953, Nix Jr. became a prominent attorney during the Civil Rights Movement.[60] This reputation led to his election to Philadelphia's Court of Common Pleas in 1968, making him the third Black to hold that position in the city.[61] In his bid for election to the state Supreme Court, Nix had the support of the Democratic Party and was able to earn 409,887 votes in Philadelphia. This was more than any other candidate and provided Nix with a majority in the state, over his Republican opponent, Judge Alexander F. Barbieri.[62]

Robert N. C. Nix, Jr.

Robert Nelson Cornelius Nix, Jr. was born in Philadelphia, Pennsylvania, on July 13, 1928. He was the son of Robert N. C. Nix, Sr., the first of Pennsylvania's African American Representatives in the United States Congress and a power-house among city Democrats. Nix's grandfather was Nelson Cornelius Nix, who was born into slavery but eventually became a minister and an academic dean of South Carolina State College at Orangeburg.

Nix, Jr was a 1946 graduate of Central High School, a 1950 graduate and valedictorian of Villanova University, and a second-generation graduate of the University of Pennsylvania Law School. He was also a postgraduate student at Temple University in Business Administration and Economics.

He served as the Chief Justice of the Pennsylvania Supreme Court from 1984 to 1996. Nix was the first African American Chief Justice of any state's highest court, and the first African American to be elected to statewide office in Pennsylvania. He served as a justice of the Supreme Court for 24 years, and was a prominent figure in Pennsylvania law and public service for more than three decades.[63]

Following the historic elections of Dr. Ethel Allen and Judge Robert N.C. Nix Jr. in 1971, the Black Political Forum continued its efforts to elect independent Black candidates to state and local offices. The Black political movement in Philadelphia was helped greatly by the National Black Political Convention of 1972, which was held in Gary, Indiana for three days beginning March 10th. I believe that this convention forged a nationwide path forward for African American politics. The National Black Convention attracted about 8,000 people from across the country. Its mission was to establish a unified political agenda that addressed poverty, unemployment, and Blacks' lack of clout within the Democratic and Republican Parties. The Philadelphia delegation was led by Hardy Williams and Richard Traylor. The keynote speaker for the Convention was Jesse Jackson, Sr., who told the delegates "We are grown. We ain't taking it no more. No more 'Yes, Boss.'" No more bowing and scraping. We are 25 million strong. Cut us in or cut us out. It is a new ball game."[64]

The convention was chaired by Richard Hatcher, the mayor of Gary who had been elected in 1968 as the first Black mayor of a major city. The delegates returned to Philadelphia inspired and determined to support more Blacks in campaigns for public office. The Black Political Forum decided to support candidates for state and federal offices, believing that the timing was right to challenge the status quo. Realistically, we did not believe that we could win all the offices we contested, but we believed that it was important to send a clear message – we will challenge party-supported candidates at every opportunity. The Black Political Forum targeted the 180th District as the next challenge, but we needed a candidate. The 180th District was represented by Francis X Rush, who had held the position for eight years in a majority Black district,

Later in 1972, the BPF convinced David P. Richardson to run for state representative in the 180th District. Richardson, who was 24 at the time, was a former Germantown High School football star and ex-gang member who in 1967 had led a demonstration in front of the school district's headquarters urging school administrators to incorporate African American history into the public school curriculum. From then on, he was regarded as the "heavyweight champion of poor people" and continued his activism in the Northwest Philadelphia community.[65] Interestingly enough, Richardson was not even registered to vote when the BPF asked him to run for office, but that was a small detail that was soon resolved.

David P. Richardson

David P. Richardson was born on April 23, 1948. He first became well-known in the political world at the tender age of 18, when he led an infamous high school protest on November 17, 1967 at Germantown High. He and a large group of 3,500 students wanted African-American history to be taught in classrooms. The police force of newly minted commissioner Frank Rizzo entered into conflict with the students, further cementing Rizzo's reputation as an aggressor. Richardson went on to become an elected member of the Pennsylvania House of Representatives in 1973, and was instrumental in organizing several movements, including a walkout on a budget meeting in 1994 that threatened to cut welfare spending. He died in office of a heart attack on August 18, 1995 at the age of 47.[66]

Richardson's opponents in the primary were Francis X. Rush, the White incumbent endorsed by the Democratic Party, and two Black ward leaders, Richard Barlow, and Gloria Llorente, who later dropped out of the race and threw her support to Richardson.[67] Richardson had worked on both of Hardy Williams' campaigns, and he employed similar strategies in his own campaign. He also brought social movement strategies from his activist background into his legislative campaign. He organized the Young Afros—a group of young people from Germantown whose goals were to eliminate gang violence, challenge police brutality and advocate for Black studies courses at the local high school—to canvass the district, hand out fliers, and attend rallies, while Richardson propagated the idea of "Black family unity and self-help".[68] His campaign also focused on increasing voter turnout throughout the district, which was filled with Black youths who had become disenchanted with Philadelphia city politics.

Richardson's presence in the race motivated many in the community to go out and vote for the first time. As one community activist told *The Bulletin*: "At last they found a reason to go to the polls. At last they found a man who could relate to them, who convinced them that they count, that they are important."[69] On Election Day, Richardson's strategy proved successful – he won a landslide victory over his Democratic opponents. David Richardson's victory was important, because it was the first time a Black independent candidate had defeated a White incumbent in Philadelphia.

In 1970, Milton Shapp was elected governor of the Commonwealth of Pennsylvania with the help of the Black Political Forum and a large turnout of Black voters. It was not surprising, then, that in 1972 the Governor appointed C. Delores Tucker as secretary of the Commonwealth – the first female African American secretary of state in the nation .As her name became a household word through the state, Tucker gained national recognition for her eloquence and imposing presence. Her appointment was another sign of the importance of the Black vote and inspired more African Americans to participate in the electoral process

C. Delores Tucker

Cynthia Delores Tucker (October 4, 1927 – October 12, 2005) was an African American politician and civil rights activist best known for her participation in the Civil Rights Movement and her stance against "gangsta" rap music. Born in Philadelphia to a minister from the Bahamas and a "Christian feminist mother," she was the tenth of thirteen children. Tucker attended Temple University and the University of Pennsylvania's Wharton School of Business. She was later the recipient of two honorary doctoral degrees, from Morris College in Sumter, South Carolina and Villa Maria College in Pennsylvania, and for this reason, she is sometimes referred to as "Dr. Tucker". In 1951, she married William "Bill" Tucker, a successful Philadelphia real estate agent, and worked in real estate and insurance sales early in her career. Tucker had a long history in the Civil Rights Movement. Early on, her civil activities included raising funds for the NAACP and participating in the 1965 march in Selma, Alabama alongside the Rev. Dr. Martin Luther King, Jr.

In 1971, Tucker became the first black female Secretary of State when Pennsylvania Governor Milton Shapp appointed her Secretary of the Commonwealth of Pennsylvania. During her tenure, she instituted the first Commission on the Status of Women. Tucker dedicated much of the last few years of her life to condemning sexually explicit lyrics in rap and hip-hop tracks, citing a concern that the lyrics were misogynistic and threatened the moral foundation of the African American community. On April 25, 2006, a state historical marker honoring Tucker was unveiled by Bill Tucker and Governor Ed Rendell in a ceremony at the State Museum of Pennsylvania, in Harrisburg.[70]

At every opportunity, the BPF continued to pursue the strategy of contesting every election. In 1974, Hardy Williams ran for congress against Robert N.C. Nix Sr. in the 2nd Congressional District of North Philadelphia. Nix Sr. was a difficult candidate to defeat; he was not only an incumbent with a host of endorsements, including that of the Democratic Party, but he was also well-recognized as the state's first Black congressman. Nix Sr. held prominent positions on a variety of Congressional committees and was involved with policies that affected the nation at large, but Williams felt Nix was not doing enough on the local level. Williams hoped to become a legislator who would focus on bringing about local change for his Philadelphia constituency. In spite of this ambition, Williams lost this campaign; however, it was a building block for the eventual defeat of Nix Sr. in 1978 by William H. Gray, III.

It was also in 1974 that John White Jr.—son of John White Sr., one of the founders of the BPF—decided to run for State Representative in the 200th District, against Gwendolyn P. Redmond and the incumbent, Rose Toll. Encompassing the neighborhoods of Mt. Airy, West Oak Lane and a portion of Germantown, the 200th District was predominantly Black, yet was represented by a White woman who was the widow of the former congressman from the 2nd District. Receiving support from the Black Political Forum, Americans for Democratic Action and the New Democratic Coalition, White ran on a platform of accountability and held a variety of social events to raise money, including chicken dinners. Stressing that he would be a candidate who was "visible, viable and vital", White aimed to address the community's displeasure with politicians who only appeared during elections but were not available to their constituents afterward.[71] Despite this strong platform, White lost to Toll by 791 votes while the other candidate, Redmond, garnered 872 votes. Arguably, had Redmond not been in the race, White would have amassed enough votes to unseat Toll in 1974.[72] The spirit of the independent Black political movement in Philadelphia had gained a lot of believers. In the year that followed, another challenge to the status quo took place when Charles Bowser decided to run for mayor with the backing of a brand new party.

John F. White Jr.

John F. White, Jr. was elected to serve as a member of the Pennsylvania State House of Representatives for the 200th District in Philadelphia in 1976. During his five-year term, he sponsored several key pieces of legislation that addressed a range of public policy concerns, including juvenile justice, prison reform, social welfare and energy issues. His leadership led to appointments to the Mass Transit and Democratic Policy Committees. In 1981, he was elected as a member of Philadelphia City Council.

During his six years as a city councilman, White served as chairman of Council's Health and Human Services Committee, where he upgraded the city's Department of Human Services, increased foster care placements and established a comprehensive Emergency Utility Fund to assist Philadelphians with heating costs.

In 1987, Mr. White was summoned back to Harrisburg and appointed secretary of the Department of Public Welfare – the Commonwealth's largest State agency. As secretary, he improved access to medical treatment for low income families and expanded health care services for children statewide. Mr. White attended West Chester University and the John F. Kennedy School of Government for Senior Executives. He is the father of three sons.[73]

In 1975, Bowser, the first Black deputy mayor under Mayor James H.J. Tate, decided to run for mayor under the newly created Philadelphia Party. The BPF asked me to organize and train the members of this new third party. This included teaching poll workers to strategically position themselves on Election Day so that they were the last people to talk to voters before they voted. It also involved teaching voters how to split their tickets, as many were only accustomed to pulling the big Democratic lever for a straight party vote during general elections. Henry Nicholas, President of 1199C, the Hospital Workers Union, reminisced about Bowser's campaign:

> In 1975...., I went with Charlie Bowser over to the Democratic City Committee to try and get him nominated. They rejected him, and we came back to my headquarters at 13th and Race Street and began our movement. Wilson Goode, Sr. had some political expertise that we didn't even know about – he knew how the ward structure worked, how the City operated. So after church on Sundays he'd come to the union hall and teach us about the ward leaders and committeemen, because we knew nothing about that.
>
> After we had been turned down by the Democratic Party, [when we decided] that we'd nonetheless run an independent candidate, we first trained ward leaders. So we had one in every ward and created our political direction. Charlie and the late Sam Evans wanted me to get politically involved because they believed that our membership organization could be the gas in the engine..... From that, the idea of the political structure emerged. We trained poll watchers and ward leaders [about] the ABCs of politics and what to do when someone comes to the polling place to vote. Goode taught us to make sure that the ballot for our candidate was on top of all other ballots and to make sure that we were the last in line so that our ballot would be on top of all the rest.[74]

As the executive director of the Urban Coalition, Bowser was credited with establishing the city's anti-poverty programs. He was well regarded in Philadelphia's Black community, and managed to attract a mass of volunteers who were willing to work on his campaign before he even announced his candidacy.[75] If elected, Bowser vowed to end the city's gang problem in less than two years.[76]

Charles Bowser

Charles Bowser was born in Philadelphia in 1931. Growing up poor in North Philadelphia, he went on to become a star fullback at Central High School. From there he went to Temple University where he earned both his bachelor's degree and a degree in law. After graduating from law school in 1957, Bowser served two years in the Army and fought in the Korean War. Returning from his tour of duty, Bowser became an attorney for the NAACP and led a successful fight to end the use of Blackface by marchers in the all-white Mummers Parade. In 1965, Bowser was named Director of the Philadelphia Anti-Poverty Action Committee (PAAC). Two years later he became deputy mayor under Mayor James H. Tate—the first Black man to be awarded the position in Philadelphia. In 1968 Bowser became Director of the Urban Coalition. For years, Bowser was a force in the city's civic and political life while mentoring and encouraging every major Black elected official. Bowser ran unsuccessfully for Mayor in 1975 and 1979.[77]

The primary candidates included Frank Rizzo; State Senator Louis Hill; and Reverend Muhammad Kenyatta, head of the Black Economic Development Conference. Rizzo easily defeated the Democratic primary candidates and faced off against Bowser—who announced his candidacy in April—and the Republican candidate, Tom Foglietta.

Bowser's campaign for mayor was built on lessons learned from Hardy Williams' 1971 campaign, and he positioned himself as an independent alternative to the "ineptness and vicious deceit of the Rizzo administration."[78] Throughout his campaign Bowser lampooned Mayor Rizzo for his upcoming plans to spend more money on the city's bicentennial celebration than he planned to spend on ending gang violence in Black neighborhoods. In an exclusive interview with the *Philadelphia Tribune*, Bowser commented, "They said they'll use $5 million for the Bicentennial, $2 million for trimming trees and only $250,000 in an effort to stop gang killings. This is absolutely diabolical. What Rizzo is saying is that trimming trees is eight times more important than saving young lives and the Bicentennial is 20 times more important. No civilized human being would set priorities like this. It's inhuman."[79]

Henry Nicholas

Nicholas has been president of the National Union of Hospital and Health Care Employees since 1981, and was elected international vice president in 1989. Nicholas began his career as a health care worker in New York City, and led organizing campaigns that built Local 1199 into a major labor organization. He has served as a member of numerous boards in the areas of rights, job training and health care.

One of ten children, Nicholas grew up in a small farming community just outside Port Gibson, MS - a town on the river that Gen. Ulysses S. Grant declared "too pretty to burn" during the Civil War. Like others in his situation, he saw the military as the way out. After his discharge, Nicholas found his way to New York, where he landed a job as an attendant at Mount Sinai Hospital.

In 1970, the union sent Nicholas to Pennsylvania to organize hospital workers. Martin Luther King's widow, Coretta Scott King, attended Nicholas' rallies for workers at Hahnemann

University Hospital and Temple University Hospital, among others. Nicholas remained a major force in Philadelphia's civic and political life.[80]

I met Frank Rizzo for the second time during that primary season. I was president and CEO of the Philadelphia Council for Community Advancement (PCCA), an organization that was helping churches and other non-profits to build homes for low and moderate income families. Rev, Cecil D. Gallup, pastor of Holy Trinity Baptist Church in South Philadelphia, asked me to accompany him to explain to the mayor the need for this type of housing in the church's neighborhood. We had an excellent meeting. However, as the meeting ended, Rizzo stood up, leaned across the table, pointed his finger at me and shouted, "I know who you are. You are not for me. You are a part of that Black Political Forum group [that's] trying to destroy me. You are not my friend, you are [my] enemy. You are only here because my friend Cecil wanted you here. You are not my friend and believe me, I am not your friend."[81] I said nothing and left the meeting. Little did I know that Rizzo and I would meet twice more after that, in the May, 1983 primary and the 1987 general election, and that I would eventually have the last word!

In spite of Bowser's strong community support, he did not win the race. However, he did manage to defeat the Republican Party nominee, Thomas Foglietta, illustrating that Bowser was seen as not just a Black candidate but as a viable and qualified candidate overall. Ultimately, what Bowser accomplished in 1975 enabled future Black mayoral candidates like me to run for office just a few years later.

In 1976, when William H. Gray, III decided to run for Congress, he sought my assistance to train poll workers and watchers, and to coordinate his Election Day activities. Gray knew of my track record with the campaigns of state representative Hardy Williams and others. Gray was a superb candidate, and we put together what we believed was a winnable campaign. In fact, with only a few divisions not counted, Gray was leading Robert N.C. Nix, Sr. by a few hundred votes, and I was so confident he would win that I called him at home and told him that he should come to the campaign office. Although the words "You have won" were never said, we both knew what I meant.

William H. Gray III

William Herbert Gray was born in Baton Rouge, Louisiana, on August 20, 1941. The son of a schoolteacher and a university president, Gray moved with his parents to Philadelphia in 1949. He attended Simon Gratz High School and went on to Franklin & Marshall College, where he graduated with his Bachelor of Arts degree in 1963.

In 1966, Gray received a master's degree in divinity from Drew Theological Seminary. He then received a master's in theology from Princeton Theological Seminary in 1970.

After his father's death in 1972, Gray assumed the role of pastor at Bright Hope Baptist Church in West Philadelphia. As his congregation grew and conditions worsened in his neighborhood, Gray was drawn into politics and took interest in the congressional district held by Robert N.C. Nix Sr., for whom he had worked during college, running in the primary election in 1976, Gray lost by a mere 300 votes. He came back in 1978 to win the position. Gray rose quickly in Congress to Minority Whip, becoming the highest ranking African-American in its history. Gray later became President of the United Negro College Fund becoming the top fundraiser in its history.[82]

However, I had underestimated the political wizardry of the state representative and ward leader, Herbert Fineman . The 22nd

Divison consisted of one senior citizen housing complex, and this single senior citizen housing center produced 509 votes for Nix and only five votes for Gray. Consequently, in the 22nd division in the 52nd ward, Nix defeated Gray by 339 votes and Gray lost by 336 votes.

This loss only set the stage for another run by Gray against Nix in 1978, in which Gray would win the congressional seat and go on to become the majority whip of the House of Representatives. In the same primary election in 1978, John F. White, Jr. ran against Rose Toll for the second time and became the second African American independent candidate to defeat a White incumbent.

Meanwhile, there was another event taking place that could have altered the course of Black political empowerment for years to come. Rizzo, the current mayor, was seeking to have the Philadelphia Home Rule Charter changed so that he could seek a third term. Rizzo convinced City Council to place a charter change question on the ballot that would have allowed him to run for a third consecutive term in 1979. Had Rizzo gotten that question on the ballot, neither Bowser's run for mayor in 1979 nor my run for mayor in 1983 would have taken place. However, Rizzo would lose the ballot question by a 2 to 1 margin.

In 1978, I was president and CEO of the Philadelphia Council for Community Advancement. Governor Milton Shapp, who had in 1972 appointed C. Delores Tucker as the first African American secretary of the Commonwealth, reached out to me to ascertain my interest in becoming the first Black member of the Pennsylvania Public Utilities Commission (PUC). Two months later I was confirmed by a vote of 48-0, and six months later I was named chairman of the PUC by the governor.

How did this appointment come about? Governor Shapp was in his last few months in office, and he wanted to appoint a member of the PUC before his term was up. However, he did not have enough votes in the State Senate to do so, because the three Black state senators from Philadelphia refused to confirm any candidate other than an African American. I had strong relationships with two of the governor's top advisors, Richard Doran and Terry Dellmuth, and they proposed my name to Shapp. I did not know the governor, and he did not know me, although I had worked on his campaign in 1970 as a part of the Black Political Forum. The three Black senators insisting on a Black appointee were Herbert Arlene, the first Black senator in Pennsylvania; Freeman Hankins, a renowned funeral director in the city, and Paul McKinney. Interestingly, these three all belonged to the inner circle of the Philadelphia Democratic Party, and were in office because they had been hand-picked by the City Democratic Committee. Nevertheless, these three senators had the courage to demand the appointment; the Governor had the boldness to make it; and I was the beneficiary.

The PUC appointment changed my life. It took me from a career managing campaigns and organizations, to a path that would ultimately lead me to become first, the managing director of Philadelphia, and then the mayor. This was the beginning of an exciting and significant period in my life.

CHAPTER 3

Eyes on the Prize: A Winning Campaign for Mayor

———◆◆———

BY THE END OF 1978, THE BLACK POLITICAL FORUM had achieved many of the purposes for which it had been organized. The training, coaching, and guidance that the BPF had provided had generated sufficient momentum to propel the Black independent political movement forward. Success had been achieved at many levels, including my appointment as chairman of the Pennsylvania Public Utilities Commission; the election of William H. Gray, III to Congress; and a solid group of Black elected officials that included Hardy Williams, David P. Richardson, Dr. Ethel Allen, Charles Hammock, John F. White, Jr. and Robert N.C. Nix, Jr. C. Delores Tucker had been appointed Secretary of the Commonwealth. John F. White, Jr. and David P. Richardson had created formidable independent political organizations in the Northwest section of the city. William H. Gray, III had created an even stronger organization in the 2nd Congressional District, and Charles Bowser had created an Independent movement as the result of his run for mayor in 1975. The Black Political Forum declared that its work was done, and felt it had set the stage for the election of the first Black mayor in Philadelphia; the odds were that Charles Bowser would be that "first".

In 1979 the stage was set for Bowser to run another campaign for mayor. This time Bowser faced off against three White men in the primary election: Congressman Bill Green; former city controller William Klenk; and former director of commerce and city representative Albert Gaudiosi. As the election evolved, it became apparent that Bowser would probably win the four-way race. Throughout the primary, the polls proclaimed that Green was the frontrunner, while others maintained that Bowser was the likely victor.[83] Some felt that the media's coverage of the primary was skewed[84]—especially Bowser, who felt that the press was unfairly playing up his race. The Green camp believed that if Klenk and Gaudiosi stayed in the race, Bowser would be the likely winner, as many polls suggested. It was then that the Green camp convinced Klenk and Gaudiosi to withdraw, leaving Green in a one on one race with Charles Bowser.

From this point on, the key to victory for both candidates was getting their respective bases of support out to vote on Election Day. For Bowser, the key was a large turnout of Black voters and the additional support of White liberals. This did not happen; Bowser lost by 30,000 votes, or as I like to put it, 15,000 persons deciding to vote another way. While Bowser lost this election, by running he had paved the way for a future Black mayor.

What would happen next had more to do with my eventual election as mayor than it did with William H. Green's narrow margin of victory in the primary. David Marston, the Republican candidate for mayor, in an attempt to woo the Black vote, announced that if elected, he would appoint a Black managing director. Charles W. Bowser, C. Delores Tucker, Samuel L. Evans, and other Black leaders threatened to withhold their support from Green unless he promised to do the same. Green agreed to make such an appointment, but he would not let the group decide who the appointee would be. The job of managing director was a coveted and integral position in the city government of Philadelphia. Right away attention turned to me. As the first Black chair of the Pennsylvania Utilities Commission, I had brought order to an out of control PUC and I was regarded as a good manager. I also got along well with Dick Doran, a long time Green advisor whose sister Patricia McKinley worked with me in Southwest Philadelphia. Incidentally, my name was at the top of the list of suitable candidates for managing director. However, there was a hitch. Lucien Blackwell, a Black City Council member, had accepted the nomination of the Consumer Party to run in the general election. This could have been a reason for Bill Green to withdraw his pledge, but Green kept the pledge and would go on to win the 1979 general election for mayor.

Lucien Edward Blackwell

Lucien Edward Blackwell (August 1, 1931 - January 24, 2003) was a United States congressman who represented West Philadelphia and parts of Delaware County, Pennsylvania from 1991 to 1995. He was a Democrat. Blackwell was born in Whitsett, in Fayette County, Pennsylvania. After attending public schools, Blackwell joined the United States Army, serving in the Korean War in 1953. Blackwell was a boxing champion during his years in the Army. He also attended West Philadelphia High School. Blackwell was a powerful Philadelphia union leader who served as president of the Local 1332, International Longshoremen's Association from 1973 to 1991. His professional political career began with election to the Pennsylvania House of Representatives, where he served from 1973 to 1975. Blackwell was best known as a vibrant member of the Philadelphia City Council from 1974 to 1991.

Blackwell was elected as a Democrat to the 102nd Congress by special election, to fill the vacancy caused by the resignation of Representative Bill Gray, and was reelected to the succeeding Congress. In Congress, Blackwell was a member of the United States House Committee on the Budget and a reliable advocate for President Bill Clinton's economic policies. Blackwell was ultimately an unsuccessful candidate for re-nomination to the One Hundred Fourth Congress in 1994, losing the primary to Chaka Fattah, and served as a lobbyist following his tenure in Congress. Blackwell self-promoted his nickname, Lucien "The Solution" Blackwell. [85]

From Outside to Inside: Managing the City

The stage was set for me to become Philadelphia's first African American managing director, the chief operating officer of service delivery in the city. Under my jurisdiction were the police and fire departments; the streets commission; licensing and inspections; public property; records; recreation; health and human services; and the water department. Throughout my time with the Black Political Forum, I had said that managing director of the city was my ideal job, never imagining that this would happen in just ten years' time. This was the top management job in the city, with one product: service to its citizens. It did not escape my notice that as the first African American to hold this position, all eyes would be on me. My mother had taught me that a first impression was a lasting one. So I had gone from an outsider knocking on the door to get in, to being on the inside and becoming responsible for many of the things that I had once complained about. I would now be capable of correcting much of what was wrong with the city's service delivery system. I was no longer the complainer, but the fixer.

My first set of interviews brought unexpected success. I asked my staff how many cars the city owned and operated. No one knew, so, in my first act as managing director, I directed that all cars assigned to city personnel be parked at Veterans Stadium and counted. That decision established me as a no- nonsense manager.

But, I knew that the African American community was primarily interested in police conduct. The Green administration was committed to fairness and justice. We issued a Deadly Force Policy that indicated when police officers were permitted to use deadly force. This was extremely unpopular with the police department; often I would come face to face with police officers and they would turn their backs to avoid saluting me. We also cancelled a police officer's class at the Police Academy and laid-off other officers. These actions resulted in pickets and demonstrations by police officers and their families.

I also worked to streamline Philadelphia's city government, to reduce the $167 million deficit that the city faced when Green took office. I had to be highly visible as well. I was always present at the scene of all the problems that the city faced.

In 1992, I wrote the following about my time as the city's managing director. "My vision of good government was one where quality management ruled. Carrying out my job, I constantly sought ways to downsize offices or to restructure departments to make them more efficient."[86] I also held weekly meetings with various groups of departmental staff in order to stay updated on each city department. "I believed my role was to be the mayor's eyes and ears in city government and on the street. I wanted to feel the pulse of the city, but I couldn't do that from my office on the sixteenth floor of the municipal services building. So besides meeting regularly with staff, I went...to where the people and the problems were."[87] Gradually these tactics paid off, and by the end of the first fiscal year of Green's administration, the city reported a $37 million surplus.[88]

In addition to focusing upon streamlining the government, I also acted as an advocate for the underprivileged, especially the homeless. I created several public programs, including a Saturday cleanup caravan called the Clean Team, and hosted town meetings to discuss the intricacies of city departments with community members. As a result of these programs and initiatives, I became quite visible within the Green administration and soon many throughout the city encouraged me to run for mayor. "You have to run for mayor next year," announced John Green, the president of the Guardian Civic League who later became sheriff, during a meeting in January 1982. "We need you....Black folks . . . liberal groups…anybody, really, who wants to end this police state in Philadelphia and the unjust treatment that so many people have endured for years. The city must be reformed. There are a lot of people out there who are ready to support you. But you've got to decide if you want to be mayor, or give in to party politics."[89]

Henry Nicholas reminisced about this time.

> Once we had stirred the bushes up, they knew there were political possibilities in the Black neighborhoods....the politics of yesterday couldn't be the politics of tomorrow, Charlie's first run showed [them] that. [When] Wilson Goode became managing director, it was clear we could make things happen…..Our membership was growing -- we were closing in at 10,000. That's a mighty base....We were able to show great power, and once Wilson Goode became managing director it was clear we could change politics. Wilson Goode had something none of the politicians had; he had a relationship and acceptability with all of the people on the religious side – with preachers. That's key if you're going to do something in a city like this.[90]

After months of speculation, I decided that I would not challenge Green in the upcoming election. After all, I owed Green for appointing me as managing director, and I felt that it would be wrong to challenge him. In 1992 I wrote, "I felt I owed him something for that. He could have picked anyone to serve in that post, but he chose me. I still didn't know how or why I had come to his attention. But I was grateful that I had and that he had shown such confidence in me."[91] After deciding not to run, I came up with a three-year plan to finish out my term as managing director and hoped to continue the post during Green's second term.

For his housing director, Mayor Green had chosen Thomas Massaro, a bright young man just 26 years old. Massaro was an aggressive advocate for the poor, especially in the housing field. Massaro hired Chaka Fattah and Curtis Jones to help him – both Fattah and Jones had distinguished themselves in running for city commissioner positions in the primary election of 1979. Even though both men had lost, they had established themselves as future leaders in the city. Ultimately Massaro fell out of favor with the mayor, and was fired. Fattah came to work in my office as my assistant. He did not want an office of his own, but instead asked for a seat outside my door in the managing director's office. His request was granted.

On January 18, 1982, my administrative aide Chaka Fattah resigned his position and announced his bid for the Democratic nomination for state representative of the 192nd District. Although the district had a significant percentage of Black voters, it had never had a Black representative and Fattah aimed to become the first. Fattah openly criticized the incumbent state representative, Nicholas A. Pucciarelli, for not devoting enough time to constituent services and never being the prime sponsor of any major legislation.[92] . Fattah aimed to defeat Pucciarelli by "knocking on every door in the district" and addressing prevalent issues, including rising crime and unemployment.[93] Fattah's strategy led him to victory in the primary, and he went on to defeat the Republican candidate, Lloyd E. Tilley, in the November general election. At age 24, Fattah became the youngest member of the Pennsylvania House of Representatives.

November 5, 1982 was also the day that Mayor Green told me he was not going to run for a second term. He looked at me and asked, "What are you going to do?" "I am going to run," I replied. Green laughed and asked if I had any money for a campaign, or a campaign strategy in mind. I replied, "No, but I am running."[94] The very next day I handed him my letter of resignation. During a press conference in my office, I announced that I would resign on November 30th. I had learned from years of political organizing that when there is a vacuum, unless one acts quickly, others will jump in and try to fill it. I felt that I was the most popular candidate and I wanted to preempt the other potential candidates, especially Lucien Blackwell and Charles Bowser, both of whom had run for mayor in 1979.

I didn't say that I was resigning as managing director in order to run for mayor, but the media and everyone else already knew that was exactly what was happening. On December 6, 1982, I officially announced my candidacy for mayor. "I am a problem solver," I said to a packed room at the Philadelphia Centre Hotel at Seventeenth Street and JFK Boulevard. "I offer to the people of our city, to all who will work with Philadelphians all over the city, someone who is committed to confronting and solving the problems we face."[95]

I am Running for Mayor: WILL YOU HELP ME?

With five months before the primary election, a host of new supporters emerged to join my campaign. Personally, I was guided by faith. Ten years later, I looked back on that time and reflected: "I didn't have a job, a political coalition, campaign manager, or anything other than my desire to serve, and faith…I had nothing to work with—no structure, no strategy. Nothing! Nothing, that is, except my faith and belief that God would see me through this campaign."[96] I remember thinking about all the hard work that had been done by others in order to bring me to this point. I knew that the work of Dr. Leon Sullivan and the 400 Black Ministers, and Sullivan's creation of the OIC, had helped to pave my way. I thought about Cecil B. Moore and all the heavy lifting he did to bring down the walls of segregated Girard College. And so many others, like Lenerte Roberts, Leonard Smalls, Hardy Williams, Charles Bowser, William H. Gray, III, Lucien Blackwell, Raymond Pace Alexander and Sadie Alexander, Marshall Shepard, Sr., C. Delores Tucker, Ethel Allen,

Octavius Catto and Edgar Campbell - whose efforts on behalf of Black Philadelphians made this day possible and brought us closer to success.

Edgar C. Campbell

Edgar C. Campbell, Sr. was born on November 11, 1902 in Savannah, Georgia. He moved with his family to Baltimore when he was 15, and then to Philadelphia when he was 19. He was a registered Republican like many other Philadelphia Blacks at the time, but after he was denied entry to the police force despite passing the exam, Campbell decided to become a Democrat.

He got into politics as "an angry young man", according to his obituary, and began his career working for Al Smith as Smith ran unsuccessfully against Herbert Hoover in the 1928 presidential election. Campbell became a central figure in Black politics in Philadelphia, although he didn't manage to actually get elected to office until 1967, when he won a seat on the Philadelphia City Council.

As a public official, Campbell was known for giving out many jobs, because according to his philosophy this was the best way to secure political influence and guarantee votes. He ended up as the clerk of Quarter Sessions Court under Frank Rizzo, after losing his bid for a third term in City Council largely due to his support of Rizzo's opponent, Pete Camiel. Campbell held this position until he was voted out in the midst of the RizzO- Goode primary competition period of 1983.

After two unsuccessful bids to take the leadership of the Fourth Ward from Chaka Fattah in 1984 and 1986, both of which he lost by only one vote, Campbell passed away on September 30, 1987 at age 84, due to complications of pneumonia. [97]

I began to design a campaign strategy to challenge my Democratic opponent, Frank Rizzo. My campaign platform was focused upon eliminating police corruption and brutality, eliminating graffiti from the city, building a new convention center, and bringing cable television to Philadelphia. Two of these issues—graffiti and cable television—had never before been addressed in a mayoral campaign; nevertheless, I was committed to pursuing them, as they were integral to the development of the city that I envisioned. I wanted a chance to put my stamp on issues I cared deeply about: the homeless, AIDS, neighborhoods, people on drugs, jobs and economic development. More than anything else, I wanted people to have access to government, and I wanted government to be an advocate for them. I knew that my campaign had to be connected to the felt needs of people, if I was going to be successful. It had to represent me and who I was. I was a child of the struggle of Black people to gain equality in a city and in a nation that had treated them as unequal for far too long. I had to level the playing field.

To staff my campaign, I hired Steve Murphy as campaign manager, and Greg Naylor as registration coordinator. Steve was a White political outsider, a trait that I valued, as I wanted someone who was independent from the city's political organizations. Greg was tasked with registering new voters and checking the status of those who were already registered. My campaign successfully registered 125,000 people—100% of the eligible Black voters at the time, a feat that I hoped would increase the likelihood of a high voter turnout. My campaign strategy was to maintain my base and get it to turn out on Election Day. One of the things I had learned from carefully analyzing the two Rizzo campaigns of 1971 and 1975 was that Rizzo never had a majority of registered voters voting for him. What he had was about 40% of the electorate, who always voted in a higher percentage than the voters who supported other candidates. I was confident that if I could get an equal level of voter turnout from my base of support, I could win. But in order to do so, I had to get at least 95% of the Black vote and 15% of the White vote. If I could get 95% of the Black vote, 15% of the White vote, and encourage equal turnout among Black and White voters, I knew that I could defeat Frank Rizzo in the primary.

Beyond voter registration, I also focused on raising money. In the first few weeks of the campaign I successfully raised approximately $50,000, which was spent on polling to assess voter preferences. The poll showed that I could beat Rizzo by 58 to 28 percent, and I used this poll as leverage to raise more money from the city's most prominent business leaders. By the end of January 1983, I had raised one million dollars. I knew then that my fundraising would be successful.

Another integral component of my campaign was the creation of "Truth Squads." These were groups of respected individuals from the community who would attend Rizzo's speeches and rallies to dispute false claims he made while on the campaign trail. The truth squads were not campaign hecklers, but well-informed citizens who would set the record straight by holding press conferences in an orderly fashion following Rizzo's events.

I also had a "Kitchen Cabinet" of three brilliant men who would advise me at critical junctures in the campaign. The three were: Dr. Maurice Clifford, president of the Medical College of Pennsylvania, who would later become my health commissioner; Dr. Bernard Watson, a vice president at Temple University, who would later become president of the William Penn Foundation and chair of the Barnes Foundation; and Richard Gilmore, executive vice president of Girard Bank, who would later become my finance director. Perhaps the single most significant contribution was made by Dr. Watson, who taught me that victory would come if I had the people "own" the campaign. To do so, he said I had to have them help me – so at the end of every speech, he told me to ask the question "Will you help me?" From that point on, every time I spoke I would state the problem and ask, "Will you help me? Will you help me?" Each time the shouts came back "Yes!" and I knew they meant it.

Later in the campaign, after Rizzo challenged me to a televised debate, I had the opportunity to set the record straight myself. Many in Rizzo's camp expected him to handily defeat me in a debate, as they only saw me as a bureaucrat who would have a hard time expressing ideas to the public. Years later, I recalled: "Because my demeanor is so low-key, some people had questioned whether or not I had media presence. Others wondered if I was too bureaucratic. Could I articulate the issues in ordinary language? Still other people worried about my stuttering." Despite the hype surrounding the debate, a few security breaches and my own anxiety, I was aptly prepared and sailed through without a problem.[98] In fact, shortly after the debate I had a realization: By God, I could win this thing; I would win this thing…I was running to become mayor of Philadelphia—and the odds were looking good that I would be elected.[99]

Years later, Bill Miller, a long-time political operative in the Northwest section of Philadelphia, reflected on those days.

> I'll tell you about the model, we had meetings in…. basements and [ran off papers] on a mimeograph, we'd get ink on our fingers. Quizzes and exams were mimeographed and we had teachers working. We had to read, we took tests, and we studied. Today you meet somebody and he says 'I did so –and someone's campaign.' When someone tells me that, I ask, 'What is it exactly [that] you did?' They put a suit on? Hung around? I did the 1983 campaign. I worked seven days a week, 13 or 14 hours a day. We achieved something no one else thought was possible. What's not talked about is that when Jesse Jackson and the Rainbow Coalition had [made] voter registration…. a mantra, we out-registered them in Philadelphia.

For Frank Rizzo, this wasn't just an ordinary campaign. I remember the first Wilson Goode fundraiser. It was January 1983 at the Top of the Bellevue. We were at the top of the Bellevue Hotel and all the power went out. Knowing Rizzo, this was no accident. We had to come down 19 flights of steps in a fire escape. I'll never forget it -Joe Certaine, myself, Greg Naylor and Jerry Cousins (the top operations people in the campaign).

We [made] the protection of Wilson Goode our personal commitment. We would have taken a bullet for him. Understand what that meant, because he was the embodiment of what this was all about for us. He and Mrs. Goode were behind me. Our eyes were big as half dollars at every landing because that's where we expected the hit to come from. And we had no guns. But we knew whatever happened, we would protect him.

In February, 1983 there was a huge blizzard. I'll say this [for] Mayor Goode, there are arguments about what kind of mayor he was, but he was absolutely the best candidate. Here's where it becomes important. During that blizzard Rizzo and [his advisors] were sitting back 'fat catting.' [Meanwhile] got....hooked....up on the radio [with WDAS}, got Greg Naylor.... a set of quarters, and Dr. Goode had a Russian Cossack hat on, and we went door to door to canvas the 60th ward, West Philadelphia, and nothing in the city was moving but the Goode campaign. We used to laugh about that hat. I'll tell you that the reason we did it, was so [Rizzo's people] would understand who they were fighting this time. We were up against Rizzo, a bigger than life person, and we wanted him to understand that whatever he put out there, we would fight it because we were going to win it.

Wilson never.... skipped a beat... No matter the craziness, he was always there.[100]

As Election Day drew nearer, I acquired more community support, particularly from Philadelphia's Black churches. Having served as a source of political mobilization during the Civil Rights movement, the Black Church and its leaders hold a prominent place in Black communities throughout the nation—Philadelphia included. Because I already had strong ties to the Church, many congregations viewed me as a native son and believed that we had the same value system. Since I held a leadership position as chair of the deacon board, I was allowed to speak in churches that normally did not open their doors to local politicians. Ministers adjusted the time they gave to their sermons to let me speak; some even cut their sermons short to let me have my say. Many of the people who campaigned on my behalf were recruited from these churches. Church coordinators became an additional source of campaign funding as they held voter registration drives and a variety of fundraisers to support my campaign. Ultimately, the high concentration of Black voters in these churches made it possible for me to mobilize the Black community through its own established institutions—something that proved invaluable throughout the campaign. To many in the Black community, this was more than a campaign – it was a crusade to make right the wrongs that had been committed against Blacks for centuries.

On Tuesday, May 17, 1983, all of these campaign tactics and strategies proved successful. Lines of Blacks gathered at their respective polling places and cast their votes for me. Many voters stood in line until 10:00 pm and others did not vote until midnight. As I surveyed the voting that day and night, I was filled with emotion, realizing that the dream of my ancestors was about to be fulfilled and that this grandson of one born into slavery was on his way to becoming mayor of the City of Philadelphia. The Black turnout was unprecedented in the city's history; I received 98% of the Black vote and approximately 22% of the White vote, giving me a win over Rizzo by almost 60,000 votes.[101] Not wanting to miss a beat after the primary, I campaigned during the summer and began to prepare for the general election, in which I would face John Egan, the Republican candidate, and Tom Leonard, an Independent.

Despite my tumultuous relationship with Rizzo, he fulfilled his Party duty and endorsed me during the general election. While his endorsement promoted unity within the Democratic Party, Rizzo also hoped that it would curry influence with me and encourage me to retain his brother as fire commissioner—something that would become a longstanding point of contention between us. Rizzo's endorsement led others to throw their support to me, including the Philadelphia Building and Trades Council, the Firefighters Union, the Teamsters and Democratic ward leaders. Throughout the rest of the general election I continued to receive prominent endorsements while publicizing my ideas for attracting more businesses to Philadelphia. Finally, on November 8, 1983, I defeated my rivals by 123,000 votes to become Philadelphia's first Black mayor.

Entering Convention Hall to acknowledge the victory, I faced a crowd of supporters who chanted my name, as I approached the microphone to shout the phrase that had become a slogan during the campaign:"Will you help me?" The crowd responded with fervent shouts of "Yes!" While the jubilance of my victory was not to be spoiled that night, I understood that even as I celebrated, there was much work to be done. In fact, I realized that my work was just beginning. So a journey that began in 1951 with a new Charter and a progressive elected official was now at a successful conclusion. A Black man had been elected mayor of Philadelphia. I did not lose sight of my new obligation to deliver on my promises. I had run campaigns for others. I had watched others achieve elected office, but I had never experienced anything like this. I was the top elected official in the city. We had climbed the mountain all the way to the top. Now it was time to deliver, and I knew that my performance had to match my promises. I asked the people to help me – and, they did!

CHAPTER 4

A Mountaintop Experience

───────◆◆───────

As I entered a new and unprecedented phase of my life as chief executive officer of a $2 billion corporation with 30,000 employees, I knew this would be the most difficult part of the journey. I felt that both Black and White Philadelphians had unrealistic expectations for my term as mayor. The Whites felt that I would keep the most difficult Blacks in line, and Blacks felt I would reverse all the wrongs committed against Blacks for the past 100 years. I knew that none of that was possible, and that whatever I did in the end would be subject to criticism by members of both communities. But, just as I had approached the work that I had done to date, I believed the key was to systematically attack the problems that detracted from the quality of life for the majority of Philadelphians. I wanted to put together the most well-qualified cabinet, but I also wanted a cabinet that was diverse in terms of both race and gender. My cabinet consisted of two Black men, two White women, one White man, and a Black female chief of staff. This cabinet makeup had been important to me ever since I had been the first Black cabinet member on a mayoral cabinet in which there had been no women. It was important to break down these barriers, but it was clear to me that this was probably the easiest of the challenges that lay ahead.

When I took office, Philadelphia had lost 150,000 jobs within the past 15 years and the city's population was experiencing a steady decline. As promised during my campaign, I aimed to restore jobs to the city by making it a more attractive place for business owners to relocate. In an effort to increase Philadelphia's marketability, I planned to spur economic development through revitalizing the city's business sector, improving Philadelphia's social services sector, and developing education and literacy initiatives throughout the city.

Revitalizing the City's Business Sector

I understood that I would need a strong commerce director to help me achieve these lofty goals. I chose David Brenner, former chair of the Chamber of Commerce, for this position. As I recalled in 1992, "David was a retired partner in a prestigious accounting firm that was well respected throughout the business community. If anyone could help staunch the flow of jobs out of the city, he could."[102] I asked Brenner to focus on the business development functions of his position, explaining that if he could bring one major business back into the city by the end of 1984, he would be considered a successful commerce director. Further alleviating Brenner's burden, I created a city representative position and appointed Dianne Semingson to handle all public relations, assigning some of the work done by the commerce director to her. By December—before I officially took office—Brenner had negotiated a deal to have Gould Electronics, a large electronics firm with branches in Philadelphia and its suburbs, consolidate its operations in the city.

In January I established the Economic Roundtable, a coalition of business leaders, to speak on behalf of Philadelphia's business community. To assess the concerns of businesses, the coalition commissioned a survey of 37,000 Philadelphia companies which revealed that quality of life issues such as crime, street maintenance and cleanliness, the city income tax and other business taxes were felt to be the most pressing problems. I promised to address these concerns as best I could, and I tried to maintain a dialogue between city government and the Economic Roundtable. "Whether or not we are successful in responding to you during my first term in office will be measured by our response to your complaints," I told the business leaders. "If any complaint you have is not responded to by the commerce section, then we are not doing our job."[103]

My next challenge was bringing a cable television system to the city. Bill Green had tried to accomplish this feat during his administration, but was stymied by disagreement with City Council over the number of cable TV vendors; while Green wanted to appoint one vendor, Council wanted to appoint one for each quadrant of the city, thereby allowing room for at least one minority firm. Deciding that it was unwise to venture into the same struggle with Council, I crafted a compromise that would allow Council to choose the four cable TV vendors who would then receive city contracts upon my approval. Council agreed to these stipulations, and cable television became a reality in the city.

Next on the agenda was eliminating graffiti in the city. Graffiti in 1983 was at an epidemic level in Philadelphia. You could not build a new building without someone writing on it. To combat the spread of graffiti into new areas of the city, I started the Philadelphia Anti-Graffiti Network, led by Timothy Spencer—a neighborhood leader from Mantua who had eliminated graffiti in his own neighborhood. Using tactics similar to what he'd done in his community; Spencer encouraged those who engaged in graffiti to turn in their spray cans and pledge to end their vandalism. Those who agreed then became graffiti artists, authorized by the city to create murals on specific buildings with free surfaces. This practice spawned the Mural Arts program that Philadelphia continues to enjoy today. Under the direction of Director Jane Golden, over 1,000 murals have been painted throughout the city. The program has been recognized as a model by the U.S. Conference of Mayors and the Ford Foundation.

Next I was presented with an opportunity to change Philadelphia's skyline. Willard "Bill" Rouse, a local developer, proposed to erect a building that exceeded the height on the William Penn statue by 400 feet. 'Liberty Place' was intended to be a downtown business complex with an innovative and sophisticated look, yet due to a traditional gentleman's agreement between developers, no building could be built in the city that exceeded the height of William Penn's hat. The rationale for this agreement was that the statue of the city's founder should remain the focal point of Philadelphia's skyline for time immemorial. But I viewed the agreement as a hindrance. Years later, I recalled,

> For me, William Penn's hat was symbolic of what was wrong with this city. As long as we were unwilling to build above William Penn's hat, we would never see beyond William Penn's hat and would remain bogged down in a tradition that had no bearing on the needs of the present or the future. We would remain the home of the Liberty Bell and the city where the Constitution of the United States was written, but we would die a slow death in the process.[104]

It is noteworthy that Edmund Bacon, who had served under four mayors as executive director of the city's Planning Commission and was once on the cover of *Time* magazine, vociferously opposed Liberty Place Towers One and Two as an "act to destroy a historical tradition that set a very fine form and discipline for Philadelphia."[105] Of course, I disagreed. Bacon served the city with great success and dignity, and he was rightly honored for his many accomplishments in his day. But this was a new day and we had to have a new vision of the city. We could not stay under the hat of William Penn and be competitive in the global economy. If we had not made that decision, there would be no Comcast Towers, Liberty One and Two, and five other skyscrapers in the city. There would be no Philadelphia skyline on national television.

When the proposal for Liberty Place was publicized, architects, builders, and developers vehemently voiced their opposition and even the public rallied against the plan. I began to doubt whether I, as the city's first Black mayor, should be the one to destroy the longstanding tradition connected with William Penn's hat; nevertheless, I proceeded to push Rouse's proposal for Liberty Place. I started by taking the members of my planning commission to the observation deck of the William Penn statue to show that from the West and Southwest sections of the city, there was no clear view of it. Therefore, the view of the William Penn statue from the west and southwest wouldn't really change with the building of Liberty Place. This visit proved effective and won the support of the commission. Next, I promoted the shops that were proposed for Liberty Place, arguing that they would be an additional source of jobs and revenue for the city. After public debate, I approved Rouse's proposal which was then approved by the planning commission and by City Council.

When the proposal for Liberty Place was approved, I realized that the city needed a strategic plan for all proposed buildings. I charged the City Planning Commission with developing guidelines for Center City in regard to development, rezoning, height limits and building standards. This plan also included a provision for the Center City District, a special services district. Businesses within the district would pay a special tax to support street cleaning, beautification and other services. Today, the Center City District continues to strive to "enhance the vitality of Center City Philadelphia as a thriving 24-hour downtown and great place to live, work or have fun."[106] Some African Americans questioned why Center City was my vital focus. My response was that Center City Philadelphia was like the heart in the body; if there is a bad heart, there can never be a healthy body. In order for Philadelphia to have healthy neighborhoods, its center must be healthy. But of course, the neighborhood and minority sectors needed attention as well.

For me, an integral part of revitalizing Philadelphia's business sector centered on involving more minorities and women. Throughout the city's history, business contracts had infrequently been made with women and minorities, and I set out to change that. I focused my energy on fully implementing the "set-aside law" which mandated that 15% of city contracts had to go to minority vendors and 10% had to go to women. Because I ensured that this law was actually being implemented and enforced, when I left office more than $500 million worth of business had been awarded to these underprivileged groups—a feat I continue to value today.

The key to economic empowerment for the African American community was opening the doors so that Black entrepreneurs could come through. I proudly embraced opening the door for Walter P. Lomax, Jr., who won a contract to provide health care in the city's prison system, and John F. White, Jr. gave Lomax a billion dollar contract when White served as secretary of welfare for the Commonwealth of Pennsylvania. At my insistence, Clarence Farmer was given a percentage of the food concession at Veterans Stadium, selling everything from hot dogs and hamburgers to beer. Patricia Corbin was my deputy managing director and became a financial advisor to the city for a contract worth $500,000 a year. She leveraged that and created Pat Corbin and Associates, becoming one of the few Black women in the country to work for herself in the financial planning industry. Willie Johnson was director of the Youth Service Commission while I was managing director; he later became the director of the Manpower Commission. I was proud to help him launch PWRT, which is now the 26th largest African American company in the country. James Wade and Wade Cable Company received one of the four franchises for cable service that we issued in 1984. Wade sold his business to Comcast, and established a thriving real estate development company in Florida. Every financing deal that we did was required to involve a Black attorney. Accordingly, five Black lawyers' names were placed in "the Red Book" – a status indicating that they were certified to do bond deals for the city.

Perhaps my stance on the Criminal Justice Center typified my insistence upon the participation of Blacks and women. I had insisted that 25% of the work involved in building the Center be set aside for Black and female contractors. The contractors sued in federal court. The federal judge asked us to negotiate. We tried, but could not make it work. I said to the contractors, "You have seventy-five percent of the work, what more do you want?" They said, "We want and deserve all of it." And I said, "Not on my watch."[107] The hole in the ground remained until I left office, and some critics saw this as symbolic of a lack of leadership on my part. I saw it as saying "No" to the racism that permeated the construction industry, both then and now. I did not have the power to force the builders to set aside 25% of the contract for Black-owned firms, but I did have the power to say "No, we are not going to build a building like that on my watch.

Improving Philadelphia's Social Services Sector

Beyond revitalizing the city's business district, I realized that providing better care for the citizens was another necessary step toward increasing Philadelphia's marketability. To improve the city's human services/social services sector, I began a crusade for human rights, focusing on the issues of AIDS and gay rights. When I took office, AIDS was primarily seen as a disease that only plagued gay males, and funding for AIDS treatment from both the state and the city was essentially non-existent. Meanwhile, Philadelphians who were diagnosed with the disease had a hard time receiving the proper treatment due to the lack of case management, home care and AIDS education. This prompted me to establish the AIDS Activities Coordinating Office—which developed an AIDS home care program and a multicultural system for AIDS case management—and the Mayor's Commission on Sexual Minorities. The creation of these groups reflected a commitment to ending discrimination based on sexual orientation within my administration. Although there was some initial backlash from former colleagues and close friends on the acceptance of homosexuality, I maintained my commitment— even marching in a Gay and Lesbian Day Parade during the Gay Pride month I proclaimed throughout the city. The infrastructure of care, services and funding provided through the city for those with HIV/AIDS under my administration has stood the test of time and can be seen in programming offered by the city to this day.

Developing Education in the City

Complementing the goal of providing Philadelphians with better social services, I also aimed to improve education in the city, specifically literacy among adults. My father could not read or count, and as a young boy I remember watching him struggle with illiteracy; even the simplest words and documents were as complex as Greek to him. Once I became mayor, I discovered that approximately 400,000 adults in Philadelphia shared the same plight as my father and had trouble completing job applications and reading street signs. The city only had 20 literacy centers where people could go to improve their skills. I began advocating for literacy and created the Mayor's Literacy Commission. The commission worked to open additional literacy centers throughout the city, and before I left office Philadelphia had 560 centers, 120 of which were equipped with computers.

Ultimately, the successes I achieved in my first term were driven by my desire to make Philadelphia a more marketable place to attract business. While these successes revitalized the city's business sector, improved its social sector and developed literacy initiatives throughout the city, Philadelphia still faced a host of problems. In fact, many of these problems evolved into tough challenges that confronted me during the remainder of my administration.

CHAPTER 5

Bad Things Happen to Good People

---◆---

IN DECEMBER OF 1982, WHEN I FORMALLY announced that I was running for mayor of Philadelphia, I stated flatly "I'm a problem solver." Little did I know that in just over two years I would have to make that statement ring true. After an extraordinarily successful first year in office, I would face six very critical issues that challenged every ounce of management skill that I possessed: (1) the collapse of the bridge used by the high speed line that connected the eastern and western suburbs; (2) the Philadelphia Eagles' announcement that the team was leaving the city to move to Phoenix, Arizona; (3) the police confrontation with the MOVE organization; (4) the 1986 blue collar workers' strike; (5) the city's deteriorating financial condition; and (6) the construction of the Criminal Justice Complex.

On September 5, 1984, we dedicated the commuter tunnel that had been under construction since the Rizzo administration. The tunnel enabled rail passengers coming from the east to connect to the western suburbs, and also to take trains to the airport. A few days prior to the dedication of the tunnel, a bridge collapsed at 8th Street and Cecil B. Moore Avenue, which stopped all trains from coming in from the east. I assembled my team and the relevant experts and challenged them to restore the bridge in 30 days. They said it was impossible and that it would take about a year to fix the bridge. So I asked the question, "If we were in a war and we needed to get supplies to the front line, how quickly could it be done?" They got the point. The bridge was completed in 30 days, in time for the Thanksgiving and Christmas shopping season. On my very last visit to the site to approve the finished project, a KYW reporter approached me and asked whether I had any comment on the news that the Philadelphia Eagles were moving to Phoenix.

So, on the very same day that I inspected the completion of the bridge in December, 1984, I received word that Philadelphia's professional football team was planning to move from Philadelphia to Phoenix, Arizona. The owner of the Eagles, Leonard Tose, had run into significant financial problems and had found that while the Philadelphia banking establishment was unresponsive to his requests for aid, the banks in Phoenix were not. I immediately contacted Mr. Tose and found that it was possible to negotiate with him. After days of negotiations, we reached a deal. The agreement called for the city to build additional skyboxes at the football stadium, to be leased to corporations, with the revenue initially going to the Eagles, but in later years going to the city. For a few weeks after this deal was announced, the media had a field day because they did not understand the deal. After I had my finance director, Richard Gilmore, explain it to members of the press, they understood that in the long run the deal would be financially lucrative for the city. The Eagles stayed, and they are still the Philadelphia Eagles today. On February 4, 2018, the Eagles won the Super Bowl and the City had the biggest celebration ever. God is a redeemer of history.

While the improvements I had made to Philadelphia's business and social services sectors were significant, my administration was not without its challenges. One challenge in particular was not program or policy-oriented; instead, it was a direct challenge with a group of people who called themselves MOVE. Originally a Black liberation group that advocated a back-to-nature lifestyle in the 1970's, MOVE maintained a home in Philadelphia for its members. The original MOVE house had been leveled to the ground by Mayor Frank Rizzo after an intense shoot- out with police on August 28, 1978 that resulted in the shooting death of Officer William Ramp. Nine MOVE members were imprisoned for his murder.

By 1984, MOVE members had relocated to 6200 Osage Avenue in West Philadelphia and turned their home into a military-style fortress, stockpiled with weapons and equipped with a bullhorn. MOVE members used this bullhorn to proclaim their ideas on what they considered to be an unjust system of local government, and to advocate for the release of their imprisoned members. As these ideas were continuously expressed in profanity-laced diatribes throughout all hours of the day and night, neighboring families became increasingly irritated. Trash and debris were strewn around the MOVE members' property as part of their back-to-nature style of living, and ultimately the environment deteriorated into conditions truly unfit for human habitation. Neighbors turned to the mayor's office for assistance, complaining in a meeting, "MOVE people have turned our neighborhood into a living hell! They are running up and down on our roofs and they have threatened people on the block. As our mayor, we want you to protect us and our children."[108]

Although I did not promise to force the group from its home, I attempted to remedy some of the neighbors' more minor complaints by removing obstructive materials from Osage Avenue's alleyways and providing mental health services for the neighbors' children through the West Philadelphia Mental Health Consortium.

Nearly a year passed without any more discussions and complaints from MOVE's neighbors. Then, in the spring of 1985, police alerted Leo Brooks, my managing director, that the group's activities were becoming more aggressive. MOVE members had a history of negative relations with the Philadelphia Police Department and often proclaimed that they felt under siege by the constant surveillance and monitoring of their home. Members of the group began building a wooden bunker on top of the home, and police surveillance recorded MOVE members using the bullhorn to threaten to kill police officers and the mayor. This activity reignited the tension between the group and its neighbors.

On Monday, May 13, 1985, police officers attempted to serve warrants to MOVE members, who had sealed themselves in their home with a stockpile of weapons. After police were unable to convince MOVE members to exit the home, shortly after 5:00 pm an explosive was dropped onto the bunker, causing a fire on the roof. By this time the MOVE men had joined the women and children in the basement of the home, in order to escape the smoke from tear gas that police had thrown into the house. After the explosion, adults and children began exiting the MOVE house to escape the oppressive smoke and debris. Watching live news reports that showed the fire raging on top of the house, I tried repeatedly to get in contact with Brooks, who was on the scene, to ask why the fire was not being extinguished by the fire department. Staff members in my office scrambled to the phones, trying desperately to reach Brooks as well. Finally, I got in touch with Leo Brooks and gave the order for the fire to be put out. Police Commissioner Greg Sambor did not carry out the command when ordered to do so by Brooks and myself. Unfortunately, by the time attempts to control the fire were actually made, it had been burning for 45 minutes and had engulfed the MOVE house as well as the other homes on Osage Avenue.

Ultimately, three city blocks were consumed by the fire, resulting in 250 people losing their homes. Eleven MOVE members died in the fire, five of whom were children. I will always remember watching the urban inferno from the television in my office. As I said eight years later, "That afternoon, watching the television screens, I saw everything that I had worked for all my life go up in smoke. I had worked my entire professional life to preserve life, to build houses, to build communities. This was totally opposite from everything I ever wanted to happen."[109]

There are many lessons to be learned from the MOVE confrontation: (1) Never send police to a situation that requires mediation rather than confrontation. (2) Make sure there are multiple ways to communicate. Today, with the advances in technology over the last thirty years, that would not be a problem; a quick text to the managing director would have ended the fire. (3) Never let people define your life's work by what happens in one day. (4) Never forget that every life should be valued and that government should do nothing to endanger life. One should never use fire as a weapon.

After the confrontation with MOVE, I had yet another challenge headed my way, this time embodied by Earl Stout. Stout was the head of District Council 33, the blue collar workers' union, and president of the John F. Kennedy Hospital in the Northeast section of the city. The hospital was completely funded from the city's health plans, but had recently experienced a financial downturn and was in serious debt. Stout came to me demanding that the city pay the union $48 million in back payments for health and welfare benefits that he had negotiated during contract talks with former mayor Frank Rizzo back in 1975. Although there were no official audits or reviews of the financial state of the hospital, Stout maintained that the city had to pay, and even took the city to court. I insisted that I wanted to see an audit of the hospital's health and welfare benefits before the city would agree to fund Stout's debt. Stout would not comply, eventually announcing that unless he received his money, the blue collar workers' union would go on strike. I knew that Earl Stout wanted a return to the "good old days" under Frank Rizzo. It was clear that Rizzo would be running against me in spirit for the next year.

Talks stalled, with Stout even refusing to meet, and on July 1, 1986, the strike began. It included all of the blue collar workers under District Council 33, and the most visible aspect involved striking sanitation workers. Scheduled garbage pickups went uncollected during the strike, resulting in trash strewn throughout Philadelphia's neighborhoods.

Months earlier, I had gone out myself to collect trash so that I could experience a day in the life of the average sanitation employee. To my surprise, I discovered that sanitation workers only worked to collect trash for three hours a day—they would load a truck, the truck would then transport the trash to the dump and during this time workers could remain idle. This experience struck a nerve within me and led me to look into getting larger trucks, in order to decrease the number of sanitation workers needed and make the trash collection process more efficient. There was a contract provision that allowed the union to veto the size of the truck – the solution to this problem would only come through contract modifications. However, my challenge now was to survive the strike so that in the future I could make contract modifications to enable the city to use larger trucks.

I read that the mayor of Atlanta, Georgia, Maynard Jackson, had survived a sanitation strike and I called him. He proposed regional dumping sites where citizens could dump their trash and private contractors could move it. I took Mayor Jackson's advice, while also providing the grounds for a court order to force the sanitation workers back to work. As suggested, I decided to set up public dumping sites where people could take their trash. The citizens removed the trash from the streets within Philadelphia's neighborhoods. But the strike still posed enough of a health hazard that grounds for declaring a health emergency could be established in court. In court, the judge ordered the sanitation workers to end their strike, but they refused.

Immediately I threatened to replace the striking workers with individuals whose names were on a waiting list for sanitation jobs. This prompted the striking workers to change their tune, and they returned to work, but not before I had renegotiated their contracts to allow for larger trash trucks without the requisite union permission.

All in all, while Earl Stout and the trash strike presented an arduous challenge, with a little cunning and the appropriate amount of confrontation, I was able to end the strike while also making the city's trash collection system more efficient. The Street Department's Sanitation Division was reduced by 1,000 employees because of the larger trucks, and the efficiency of collections increased.

Now that I had climbed to the Mountaintop and spent three years running the city, the question was, had I done a good enough job for people to affirm me in office, or was this journey going to end in disappointment for those of us who had sought to get here? Two years after the MOVE confrontation and one year after the blue collar workers' strike, I was running for reelection. And the year1987 would be the most challenging of all. The Black church folk who had supported me in 1983, supported Ed Rendell for governor and had extracted a promise from him that if he ran and lost, he would not run against me for mayor. In the primary of 1987, Rendell did not keep his word and announced that he would challenge me in the primary. Many felt that Rendell could defeat me, and that if he could not, certainly Frank Rizzo could.

Rizzo had switched parties and was now running in the Republican primary election to face me in November, should I win the Democratic Primary. I received some more bad news - my media advisor, Neil Oxman, who had done all of my advertising in 1983, was leaving to join the Rendell campaign The question in the minds of many was, given the challenges of MOVE and the blue collar workers' strike, would the coalition I had built in 1983 hold together for this election?

Although not as passionate as it had been during the1983 race, my coalition held together in my second mayoral primary, in which I received 98 percent of the Black vote and 12 percent of the White vote. I was able to defeat Rendell by a margin of 58% to 42%, the exact percentage by which I had defeated Rizzo four years earlier. But I knew that the race against Rizzo in the November election would be much more challenging. After all, the general election would add about 200,000 Republicans who could vote for Rizzo in November. Six months later, in a very tough general election, I defeated Frank Rizzo by more than 30,000 votes. So in one year, I had defeated Ed Rendell, who would later become a two term governor and chair of the national Democratic Party, and Frank L. Rizzo, who only had been defeated once before, by me, in 1983. For me the mayoral journey continued. And the work we set out to do was affirmed by the citizens of the City of Philadelphia.

As I neared the end of my two terms as mayor, the finances of the city were deteriorating. This was not a sudden reality, it had been in the making for about ten years. Before that, Philadelphia had experienced a long decline in its economic base and over the past 30 years had lost 400,000 residents. To make things worse, the crack cocaine epidemic in the city and nationwide had caused crime in the city to rise exponentially. In my final year it became obvious to me that we had to make some drastic cost-saving decisions, including program cuts and layoffs. We had to do some short-term borrowing that I believed would have taken us to the end of the term, but City Controller Jonathan Saidel refused to sign the Tax Anticipation Notes (this is money borrowed in anticipation of the following spring's tax revenues). There has never been another time in the history of the city, before or since, when this has taken place. The controller's refusal to sign was a political decision, and was agreed to by the incoming Rendell administration. Earlier in the year the State had created the Pennsylvania Intergovernmental Cooperation Authority (PICA), which was charged with restoring financial stability and achieving balanced budgets in Philadelphia. All of this was part of the incoming administration's strategy, not only to balance the budget, but to force the municipal unions into concessions that would enable Mayor Rendell to claim a financial turnaround for the city. It was a good strategy, and it worked.

CHAPTER 6

We Mastered the Process, but Not the Mission

As I was completing my second term in office, the primary election came around, and the question on everyone's mind was, would a Black person succeed me as mayor? There were three Black candidates who had expressed interest in running – James Stanley White, my former managing director; George Burrell, a strong ally of William H. Gray, III; and Lucien Blackwell, who had sought the office in 1979 and was a long- time Council member. Our best efforts failed to get these three men to agree on a process by which two of them would withdraw, therefore setting up a one on one race against Ed Rendell, who was again running for mayor after his loss to me four years earlier.

Rendell was considered the favorite because there were three Black candidates in the race. After we failed to convince two of the Black candidates to drop out, I decided to support George Burrell for mayor, although my heart and soul were with James Stanley White. My rationale was that Burrell had the best chance to win, and per- haps my endorsement of Burrell would cause White and Blackwell to withdraw from the race. James Stanley White withdrew and supported Lucien Blackwell. With the Black vote divided, Rendell went on to win the primary and the general elections in November. This lack of success in 1991 was also a product of the lack of camaraderie among the Black candidates, a trend that had been intensifying since my election.

I concluded my two terms as mayor of Philadelphia feeling proud of my time in office, and with great pride that I had left the city in a much stronger position than it had been in for thirty years. The strength of a city is not just related to its financial position, although that is an important part. I had eliminated graffiti by creating the Anti-Graffitti Program and the Mural Arts Program. I had created programs for AIDS patients and the homeless. I had changed the skyline and created the Center City District. I had leveled the playing field for Blacks and women in government. I had paved the way for at least six major Black-owned businesses to become million dollar companies – the businesses of Walter Lomax, Willie Johnson, Patricia Corbin, Clarence Farmer, Will Daniels and the law firm of Archie and Atkinson. I had also placed the names of five Black attorneys in the Red Book: Robert Archie, Nolan Atkinson, Leon Tucker, Rotan Lee and George Burrell. No other city in the U.S. had as many Black attorneys in its Red Book. The Red Book authorizes attorneys to participate in governmental issuance of financial bonds. I had appointed competent leaders who would advance to major leadership roles in the city. I felt I had conquered the Mountaintop twice, and had done well by those who paved the way to get me there.

Mayor Rendell went on to form a partnership with John F. Street, the incoming president of City Council. Their partnership and the city's successes during the Rendell years pushed John F. Street to the forefront as a potential mayoral successor to Rendell. In the primary election of 1999, three Black candidates were all in the race: John F. Street; John F. White, Jr., the former state secretary of welfare; and Dwight Evans, chair of the House appropriations committee

There were also two White candidates – Martin Weinberg, who was Rizzo's city solicitor and campaign manager, and Happy Fernandez, former City Council Member-at-Large. Together the three Black candidates won 61.8% of the vote, with 25% of that vote being cross-over votes from White Philadelphians. Although Street received just over one-third of the vote, the result showed the power of the Black electorate when combined with crossover voting from the White community; it showed that a well-financed Black candidate could win. John Street would go on to win the general election and become the second Black mayor in the history of Philadelphia. The election of John Street in 1999 signaled the end of the era of independent elected officials who had deep roots in social action and the civil right movement.

John F. Street

John Franklin Street was born into rural poverty in 1945 in Norristown, Pennsylvania, where he worked on his parents' small farm. He graduated from Conshohocken High School and then studied English at Oakwood College in Huntsville, Alabama. In 1975 he gained a Juris Doctorate from Temple University Law School, working as a street vendor to pay tuition. Following his graduation, Street undertook clerkships with the Common Pleas Court and the United States Department of Justice. In his first professional job, Mayor Street taught English at an elementary school and, later, at the Philadelphia Opportunities Industrialization Center. He also practiced law privately prior to entering into public service.

Street began his public career as a community activist. He was then elected to Philadelphia City Council in 1979. For nearly 20 years, Street represented the city's 5th Council District. Diverse economically and racially, the 5th District comprises 11 wards in North Central Philadelphia and Center City and encompasses some of the city's most affluent addresses, such as Rittenhouse Square, as well as some of the city's most depressed areas. Street was chosen unanimously by members of the council, backed by both Democrats and Republicans, to serve as its president in 1992, and again in 1996. During his time as City Council president, Street worked to promote community policing and for tougher gun laws. As president, Street worked closely with the administration of Mayor Ed Rendell, who later served as Pennsylvania's Governor. Elected in 1999 and again in 2003, Philadelphia's Mayor John F. Street carries with him a work ethic derived from his impoverished childhood. Street has participated in the Democrat-led turnaround of the city over several decades as both City Council president and mayor. Having provided jobs, regenerated neighborhoods, and halted educational decline, Street saw technology as the key to a more prosperous Philadelphia.[110]

The 2007 mayoral primary consisted of three Black candidates: Dwight Evans; Chaka Fattah; and Michael Nutter, a member of City Council in the 4th District. There were also two White candidates: Tom Knox, an insurance business executive; and Bob Brady, a member of Congress in the 1st District and Democratic Party chair since 1987. Nutter would win this race with a little over one-third of the vote. The success of my mayoral campaigns in 1983 and 1987 was due to the presence of a unified Black electorate, which neither Street nor Nutter had in their primary wins. Michael Nutter would go on to win the general election in November, 2001 and become the third Black mayor of Philadelphia. Nutter's election made Philadelphia the only one of the top ten U.S. cities to have had more than one Black mayor. Philadelphia has had three African American Mayors.

Like Street, Nutter did not come out of the social action and protest movement. Mayor Nutter had substantial support from White voters, by far exceeding the level of White support that Street and I had received. This indicated that Black candidates running for mayor in the future could use the Nutter Model. Nutter ran a broad-based campaign to appeal to all voters. This resulted in his receiving 40% of all White votes, more than double the White votes received by any other Black candidate.

Michael Anthony Nutter

Michael Anthony Nutter (born June 29, 1957) was the 98th mayor of Philadelphia. He is the third African American to hold the position. Elected on November 6, 2007, he was re-elected to a second term on November 8, 2011. He is a previous member of the Philadelphia City Council from the 4th District, and has served as the 52nd Ward Democratic leader since 1990. Mayor Nutter also served as the president of the United States Conference of Mayors from June 2012 to June 2013.

Nutter graduated from The Wharton School at the University of Pennsylvania in 1979 with a degree in business. During his sophomore year in college, he started working as a DJ at Club Impulse in Philadelphia, where he was known as Mix Master Mike. After graduating college, Nutter began to work at Xerox, and then at an investment banking firm. While in office, Mayor Nutter occasionally has shown off his skills as a DJ and singer.

Michael Nutter is a member of the Mt. Carmel Baptist Church in West Philadelphia. Nutter, then the leader of the 52nd ward of Philadelphia, initially challenged Democratic incumbent Ann Land for a seat on the Philadelphia City Council in 1987. Though ultimately unsuccessful in his initial bid, Nutter defeated Land in a rematch four years later. His district included Wynnefield, Overbrook, Roxborough, Manayunk, East Falls and parts of North Philadelphia, West Philadelphia, and Mount Airy. In February 2003, Nutter was elected chairman of the Pennsylvania Convention Center Authority Board at the urging of former Senator Vincent Fumo.[111]

In addition to the mayor's office, African-Americans now held many other influential elected positions in Philadelphia and the surrounding area: they held seats on the City Council; in the state House of Representatives; in the state Senate; in the United States Congress; served as school superintendents and held other political leadership positions. . For the most part, however, while these candidates had mastered the process of winning, many of them forgot the greater purpose for which they were running. They went from being reformers, to becoming ordinary politicians – more concerned about re-election than about reforming bad policies and advocating for the needs of the people. They became those whom they had replaced.

CHAPTER 7

The Way Forward: Black Voting Matters

———◆———

PHILADELPHIA NOW HAS THE HIGHEST NUMBER OF African American elected and appointed officials in its history. At present, City Council has eleven non-White members: one Latino, two Asians and eight African Americans. Its president and majority whip are both African Americans. Philadelphia's third African American mayor served two terms office. City Council has its third Black president. The journey toward Black political empowerment in the City of Philadelphia has marched steadily upward since the founding of the Black Political Forum in 1968. As I pointed out in the last chapter, African Americans have mastered the process of running for office and getting elected in Philadelphia. All three Black mayors can point to solid achievements in office that compare favorably with those of Philadelphia's White mayors over the last 64 years.

Legislators and council members have also done great work. But I believe that the work of the Black Political Forum did not go far enough, and perhaps ended prematurely. I now believe that the Forum should have shifted its focus from getting Blacks elected, to teaching Black candidates how to effectively navigate through the legislative process to get bills passed and implemented. The "Way Forward" for Black elected officials is a more effective use of their positions. It is imperative that today's Black politicians see elected office not an end in itself, but as a vehicle for getting things done; a vehicle for the political and economic empowerment of people who were excluded from the system until just 50 years ago. The purpose of the struggle and the journey has always been to place African Americans in positions where they could become agents of economic and political change, where they could advocate for a population of people who have systematically been left out in the City of Philadelphia. There is a need for a moral compass to guide today's elected officials. There is a need for politicians to feel more passionate concern for those who are poor and marginalized. There is a need for politicians to be bold in confronting the wrongs in today's society. Advocacy for the people is essential. There are "Ways Forward." Let me suggest five things that must be done to recapture the spirit that propelled me into the mayor's office:

(1) Candidates must examine their reasons for seeking elective office. If they are motivated only by the prospect of personal victory, they should not run. If there is no larger purpose attached to the process, they should not seek office. They must be purpose-driven and passionate about making this a great city.

(2) The electorate must be more selective with its votes. . Candidates must be evaluated. Their entire backgrounds must be examined. If they don't have track records of unselfish service, then elected office is not the job for them. If they have made no contribution to the community, it is not likely that they will make one in elective office.

(3) An organization similar to the Black Political Forum should be established to evaluate those who run for office, and make these evaluations available to members of the community. A desire to be an elected official is not a qualification for running for office. This organization should interview candidates and hold them accountable to ensure that their performance matches their promises. It is obvious that many elective officials find it difficult to navigate through the many complex issues they face. More training is needed. This is true especially in the area of ethics. Some get caught in ethical issues that result in embarrassment and arrest because they have difficulty in distinguishing between right and wrong actions. Training could decrease the chances of this happening.

(4) Each Black candidate running for office should have a sense of the history of the struggle for Black political empowerment, both here in the City of Philadelphia and across the nation. Acquiring a sense of history and struggle should move these candidates from a self-absorbed agenda to a purpose-driven one.

(5) To be effective, candidates must be aware of the events and personalities in the past that have made it possible for them to seek office. They must see these connections between the past and the present and be mindful of those who have struggled so that they might have the opportunity to serve the public today. Connecting the past to the present is essential to political success.

If today's Black politicians will follow these recommendations, they could rekindle the spirit of the 1960s,'70s and '80s that transformed the landscape of Black empowerment in Philadelphia, and could propel Blacks even further forward, to fulfill the dreams of the pioneers who made it all possible.

The Primary Election of May 2015 suggests that Black empowerment in Philadelphia politics may take on a different form. In the Democratic Primary Election for mayor in May 2015, some were surprised by the margin of victory, including James F. Kenney. Kenney, a White man, became the first Democratic nominee for mayor to receive more than 50% of the vote in the Primary Election since I ran for mayor in 1983 and 1987.

In a field of six candidates, reaching the fifty percent mark was significant. It was achieved with a broad-based coalition of unions, African American political leaders, LBGT supporters and others. Kenney received more African American votes than any other candidate. He received 46% of the Black vote and 70% of the White vote. Together, Kenney and his opponent Lynne Abraham received nearly 80% of the White vote. This demonstrates that African Americans are more likely to reach across racial lines to vote for Whites than Whites are willing to reach across racial lines to vote for a Black when White candidates are in the race. Michael Nutter received a higher percentage of White votes than any other Black candidate running for Mayor in a Primary Election in Philadelphia.

So, what does all of this mean for Black electoral empowerment in the City of Philadelphia? When Jim Kenney took office in January 2016, it meant that only one of the top ten U.S. cities had a Black mayor. The question is, how will Philadelphia's other Black political leaders use their influence to benefit the larger African American community? Moreover, how will the considerable influence of unions and labor leaders limit that influence? And, how will these often conflicting interests impact the future of Black political empowerment in Philadelphia?

Philadelphia has eleven persons of color on City Council – a clear majority. In 1968, there were three persons of color on City Council. But beyond that, it is not clear what the future looks like. There are fewer top level African Americans in key positions in the executive branch than there were when I left office in 1992. Here are the highlights: only 36.6% of the City population and 39% of the City government is White, but 49% of exempt employees and 60% of executive exempt employees are White – including 60% of the Commissioners and Directors and 69% of the Cabinet (11 of 16) .. African Americans are the largest population group in the City with 665,000 people. Yet there are more questions than answers. The 2015 mayoral election may have changed Philadelphia politics as much as my election to mayor did in 1983. With the increase in the Latino population in the city and the return to the city of young White families, Philadelphia probably has seen its last African American mayor elected solely on the strength of the African American community.

In the election of 2015, the majority of eligible voters did not vote. Jim Kenney received 126,000 votes with a 27% turnout. Apathy was the most broad-based coalition. In 1983, I won the mayor's office with 425,000 votes, with a voter turnout of over 70%. In the end, empowerment is about participation. BLACK VOTING MATTERS!

AFTERWORD

When W. Wilson Goode, Sr. left office as the first African-American mayor of Philadelphia in 1992, he was immediately succeeded by Edward G. Rendell – and then, the city elected two successive African-American Mayors, John F. Street and Michael A. Nutter (2000-2008, 2008-2016). When Goode left office, John Street was elected president of Philadelphia City Council by a majority-white legislative body, and during Street's subsequent tenure as mayor, the racial diversity of that body did not change much. The 2007 and 2011 municipal elections did change the racial composition of Council, which came to include eight African-Americans, the first Latina member, and the first Asian-American member. The growth in that diversity can be attributed to several factors, including general demographic changes in the city's population, specific political alliances, and legislation enacted to change the racial composition within specific City Council districts that had growing populations of people of color. In short, as Philadelphia became a city with people of color as its majority, the elected representation eventually began to reflect that change, both naturally and by design, linked to decades of independent political organizing and strategizing.

In terms of diversity, there has definitely been an increase in the number of local elected officials who are people of color. To analyze the real impact of that change, we must also examine whether there has been an improvement in the quality of life in communities where there are a majority of people of color. Sadly, the same racial disparities still persist with regard to health, education, and economic opportunity and suggest that the story of 21st century Philadelphia is still a tale of two cities – but there has been some progress in the last half-century.

For example, the Goode mayoral administration (1984-92) did more contracting with businesses owned by people of color than every other preceding administration combined. Unfortunately, even after two successive African-American mayors (2000-16), businesses owned by white males still receive roughly seventy percent of Philadelphia's total contracting dollars. The city now conducts an annual disparity analysis to determine what the appropriate level of utilization of minority-owned firms should be, based upon the availability of disadvantaged businesses to provide goods and services to the city - but the implementation of that policy still falls short. There has been some improvement since the Rendell years (1992-2000, when over ninety percent of Philadelphia's contracting dollars were going to businesses owned by white males. This is only one small example of the racial disparities that elected officials can affect through sound public policy. The question then becomes whether having an increase in the number of elected officials who are people of color has translated into more effective public policy to address the city's racial disparities.

The minimal goal should be simple fairness in the expenditure of public funds. A more ambitious goal would be greater investment in racial equity. The ultimate goal should be to eliminate all racial disparities.

The issue of Black political empowerment should never have simply been about electing Black people, but about creating more racial equality where inequalities exist. The purpose of Black political empowerment was to overcome racial disadvantages through the leverage of electoral strength, but not by empowering elected representatives who are not trained to be effective public policy makers – this approach may bring about quantity, but not necessarily quality.

The stark difference between Wilson Goode and most other Philadelphia elected officials is that Goode was a trained public administrator - both academically and professionally - and his service as the city's first Black managing director proved that people of color could govern at the highest level. Before his historic election as mayor, Goode's work as the second-highest ranking administrator in city government changed the game forever - and after his election, he brought even more diversity into Philadelphia's government in a dramatic way. The Goode Administration increased the percentage of people of color in city government to over forty-seven percent, and that percentage has since increased to almost sixty percent.

The enduring legacy of Black political empowerment in Philadelphia is not just limited to these dozens of Black elected officials, but rightfully extends to the thousands of non-elected public servants throughout Philadelphia government who ensure that there is more fairness and equality today in the delivery of city services, to improve the quality of life in communities of color and in the community at large. It's not just about electoral victories; it's about effective government – to improve the quality of life for everyone!

W. Wilson Goode, Jr.
The Honorable W. Wilson Goode, Jr. served 16 years as City Councilman at Large and is now Chief Policy Advisor to the Philadelphia City Council.

ACKNOWLEDGMENTS

I want to acknowledge Professor Dr. John J. Dilullio, Jr. and Joseph P. Tierney of the Robert D. Fox Leadership Program. I also want to thank three student research assistants from the Fox School: Ethan Lowens, Mark Paraskevos and Mikecia Witherspoon for their research and interviews.

I want to acknowledge some key people who helped me on my journey in becoming mayor: Richard Doran and Terry Dellmuth who recommended me to Governor Milton Shapp to become a Commissioner of the Pennsylvania Public Utility. There were three courageous Black Senators from Philadelphia who refused to support any candidate for the Commissioner position who was not Black. Senators Herbert Arlene, Freeman Hankins, and Paul Mckinney.

I want to thank Charles Bowser, Samuel L. Evans and C. Delores Tucker who paved the way for my being appointed as Managing Director by refusing to support the winner of the Primary in 1979 unless he agreed to appoint a Black Managing Director.. I also want to thank former Mayor William H. Green, III for breaking the barrier and appointing me as the first African American managing director and cabinet officer.

I want to thank Dr. Bernard C. Watson for his encouragement to do this book and writing the Foreword.

I want to thank Shirley B. Hamilton, my executive assistant for her editing and typing, and thanks to Amarty Daniel, staff administrator, for her editing and typing.

I want to thank my three children: Muriel Goode Trufant, W. Wilson Goode, Jr. and Natasha P. Goode for their support in shaping this history.

Finally, I want to thank my wife Velma, of 57 years, for daily encouragement of this work.

REFERENCES

(article on lack of Black political power in spite of Black voters electing Mayor Tate in 1963 and 1967, supports claims made by Wilson Goode in interview/motive for creating BPF)
Norris Charges Intelligent Negroes Letting Extremists Speak for Them Politically
Norris, Austin
Philadelphia Tribune (1912-2001); Feb 22, 1969;
ProQuest Historical Newspapers: Philadelphia Tribune (1912-2001)

Charles Bowser Forms 3rd Party; Will Run for Mayor in November
Philadelphia Tribune

(article mentions the lack of women in City Council)
Women in Politics: 2nd Annual Banquet of Blk. Councils Attracts Political and Civic Leaders
Robinson, Mamie
Philadelphia Tribune (1912-2001); Mar 27, 1971;
ProQuest Historical Newspapers: Philadelphia Tribune (1912-2001)
pg. 14

ENDNOTES

1 Goode Research Report, May 2015.

2 Ibid.

3 Ibid.

4 Ibid.

5 Ibid.

6 Ibid.

7 Ibid.

8 Ibid.

9 Ibid.

10 "Rochester Riot Timeline." *PBS*. PBS, n.d. Web. 29 Oct. 2013. <http://www.pbs.org/independentlens/july64/timeline.html>.

11 Goode Research Report May 2015

12 Ibid

13 Countryman, Matthew. *Up South: Civil Rights and Black Power in Philadelphia*. Philadelphia: University of Pennsylvania, 2006. Print.

14 Goode Research Report, May 2015.

15 Ibid.

16 Ibid.

17 Ibid.

18 Ibid.

19 Girard College website. < http://www.girardcollege.edu>.

20 Kativa, Hilary S. "The Desegregation of Girard College." *Civil Rights in a Northern City: Philadelphia*. Temple University, n.d. Web. 06 Nov. 2013. <http://northerncity.library.temple.edu/content/collections/desegregation-girard-college/what-interpretative-essay>.

21 Goode Research Report, May 2015.

22 Ibid.

23 "Roberts Declares He's In Mayor Race to Stay." *The Philadelphia Tribune* 2 May 1967: n. pag. *ProQuest Historical Newspapers*. Web. 6 Nov. 2013.

24 Ladeau, Marie. "Specter's Team Wins in GOP Election Tate Defeated Hemphill by 71,771." *The Philadelphia Tribune* 20 May 1967: n. pag. *ProQuest Historical Newspapers*. Web. 6 Nov. 2013.

25 "Cleric Seeking Post of Mayor." *The Philadelphia Tribune* 2 Sept. 1967: n. pag. *ProQuest Historical Newspapers*. Web. 8 Nov. 2013

26 All-NegroParty Headed by Moore." *The Philadelphia Tribune* 18 Mar. 1967: n. pag. *ProQuest Historical Newspapers*. Web. 8 Nov. 2013.

27 Saunders, John. "Mayor Tate Owes His Victory to Negro Vote." *The Philadelphia Tribune* 11 Nov. 1967: n. pag. *ProQuest Historical Newspapers*. Web. 8 Nov. 2013.

28 Countryman, Matthew. *Up South: Civil Rights and Black Power in Philadelphia*. Philadelphia: University of Pennsylvania, 2006. Print.

29 "Cleric Seeking Post of Mayor." *The Philadelphia Tribune* 2 Sept. 1967: n. pag. *ProQuest Historical Newspapers*. Web. 8 Nov. 2013.

30 Ibid.

31 Dionne, E. J., Jr. "Watch Those Guys." *The Washington Post.* The Washington Post, 24 May 2005. Web. <http://www.washingtonpost.com/wp-dyn/content/article/2005/05/23/AR2005052301337_pf.html>.

32 "Tate Names Bowser Deputy Mayor at $18,000 a Year: Tate Names Bowser As Deputy to Mayor." *The Philadelphia Tribune* 3 June 1967: n. pag. *ProQuest Historical Newspapers.* Web. 7 Nov. 2013.

33 Goode Research Report, May 2015.

34 Saunders, John. "Mayor Tate Owes His Victory to Negro Vote." *The Philadelphia Tribune* 11 Nov. 1967: n. pag. *ProQuest Historical Newspapers.* Web. 8 Nov. 2013.

35 White Jr., John F. Interview with Ethan Lowens. Personal interview. Philadelphia, July 12, 2013.

36 Goode Research Report, May 2013.

37 Ibid.

38 Ibid.

39 Norris, Austin. "Norris Charges Intelligent Negroes Letting Extremists Speak for Them Politically." *The Philadelphia Tribune* 22 Feb. 1969: n. pag. *ProQuest Historical Newspapers.* Web. 21 Feb. 2014.

40 Ibid.

41 Goode Research Report, May 2013.

42 White Jr., John F. Interview with Ethan Lowens. Personal interview. Philadelphia, July 12, 2013.

43 White Jr., John F. Interview with Ethan Lowens. Personal interview. Philadelphia, July 12, 2013.

44 Countryman, Matthew. *Up South: Civil Rights and Black Power in Philadelphia.* Philadelphia: University of Pennsylva-

nia, 2006. Print.

45 Goode Research Report, May 2013.

46 Ibid.

47 White Jr., John F. Interview with Ethan Lowens. Personal interview. Philadelphia, July 12, 2013.

48 White Jr., John F. Interview with Ethan Lowens. Personal interview. Philadelphia, July 12, 2013.

49 White Jr., John F. Interview with Ethan Lowens. Personal interview. Philadelphia, July 12, 2013.

50 Ibid.

51 Ibid.

52 Ibid.

53 Haynes, Pamala. "Rizzo's Big Victory: How, Why and What It Means: Black Mayor Hopes Are Dimmer." *The Philadelphia Tribune* 22 May 1971: n. pag. *ProQuest Historical Newspapers.* Web. 20 Nov. 2013.

54 Haynes, Pamala, and Ruth Rovner. "St.Thacher Longstreth Banking On Black Vote to Beat Rizzo." *The Philadelphia Tribune* 22 May 1971: n. pag. *ProQuest Historical Newspapers.* Web. 21 Nov. 2013.

55 "Longstreth to Make Pitch to Black Political Forum Rizzo Decides to Warm Bench." *The Philadelphia Tribune* 31 July 1971: n. pag. *ProQuest Historical Newspapers.* Web. 21 Nov. 2013.

56 Wikipedia??

57 Lear, Len. "Moore Comes Out 'Fighting' For Longstreth, Raps Rizzo." *The Philadelphia Tribune* 2 Oct. 1971: n. pag. *ProQuest Historical Newspapers.* Web. 21 Nov. 2013.

58 Rhodes, John. "Rev. Leon H. Sullivan Endorses Longstreth for Mayor: Rizzo's Election Will Divide City, Minister Asserts." *The Philadelphia Tribune* 23 Oct. 1971: n. pag.*ProQuest Historical Newspapers*. Web. 21 Nov. 2013.

59 Haynes, Pamala. "McIntosh Beaten by Anti-Rizzo Tide, Dr. Allen Says." *The Philadelphia Tribune* 9 Nov. 1971: n. pag. *ProQuest Historical Newspapers*. Web. 21 Nov. 2013.

60 "R. N. C. Nix Jr., 75, Groundbreaking Judge." *The New York Times*. N.p., 26 Aug. 2003. Web. 3 Dec. 2013. <http://www.nytimes.com/2003/08/26/us/r-n-c-nix-jr-75-groundbreaking-judge.html>.

61 "Hundreds of Officials and Citizens See Young Nix Take Judgeship Oath." *The Philadelphia Tribune* 6 Jan. 1968: n. pag. *ProQuest Historical Newspapers*. Web. 3 Dec. 2013.

62 Saunders, John. "Blacks Voted Against Frank Rizzo But Supported His Running Mates." *The Philadelphia Tribune* 6 Nov. 1971: n. pag. *ProQuest Historical Newspapers*. Web. 21 Nov. 2013.

63 Goode Research Report, May 2013.

64 Ibid.

65 Eshelman, Russel E., Dianna Marder, and Peter Nichols. "State Rep. David P. Richardson Jr., 1948-1995 An Activist And A Gentleman." *The Inquirer* [Philadelphia] 19 Aug. 1995: n. pag. *Philly.com*. Web. 4 Dec. 2013. <http://articles.philly.com/1995-08-19/news/25707304_1_richardson-police-brutality-heart-disease>.

66 Goode Research Report, May 2013.

67 Lear, Len. "Germantown Activist Runs for Legislature." *The Philadelphia Tribune* 7 Mar. 1972: n. pag. *ProQuest Historical Newspapers*. Web. 4 Dec. 2013

68 Countryman, Matthew. *Up South: Civil Rights and Black Power in Philadelphia.* Philadelphia: University of Pennsylvania, 2006. Print.

69 "Blacks Celebrate Victories Over 'Machine' in Legislative Races." *The Bulletin* [Philadelphia] 27 Apr. 1972: n. pag. Print.

70 Goode Research Report, May 2013.

71 "White Endorsed by Political Alliance." *The Philadelphia Tribune* 18 May 1974: n. pag.*ProQuest Historical Newspapers.* Web. 12 Dec. 2013.

72 Lear, Len. "John White, Jr. Is Trying To Unseat Rose Toll Again." *The Philadelphia Tribune*10 Feb. 1976: n. pag. *ProQuest Historical Newspapers.* Web. 12 Dec. 2013.

73 Goode Research Report, May 2013.

74 Nicholas, Henry. Interview with Ethan Lowens. Personal interview. Philadelphia, July 10, 2013.

75 Bennett, Paul. "Bowser for Mayor Club Opens in W. Philadelphia." *The Philadelphia Tribune* 14 Dec. 1974: n. pag. *ProQuest Historical Newspapers.* Web. 18 Dec. 2013.

76 Downing, Margo. "Bowser Vows to End Gang Violence If Elected Mayor." *The Philadelphia Tribune* 28 Dec. 1974: n. pag. *ProQuest Historical Newspapers.* Web. 18 Dec. 2013.

77 Goode Research Report, May 2013.

78 "Charles Bowser Files for Mayoralty Contest." *The Philadelphia Tribune* 22 Mar. 1975: n. pag. *ProQuest Historical Newspapers.* Web. 19 Dec. 2013.

79 Ibid.

80 Goode Research Report, May 2013.

81 Ibid.

82 Ibid.

83 Davis, Jim. "Mayoral Hopeful Charles Bowser Needs a Heavy Voter Turnout." *The Philadelphia Tribune* 15 May 1979: n. pag. *ProQuest Historical Newspapers*. Web. 3 Jan. 2014.

84 Bervine, Junius, and David Weeks. "The Media, Mayoral Campaign and Charles Bowser." *The Philadelphia Tribune* 13 Apr. 1979: n. pag. *ProQuest Historical Newspapers*. Web. 3 Jan. 2014.

85 Goode Research Report, May 2013.

86 Ibid.

87 Ibid.

88 Ibid.

89 Ibid.

90 Nicholas, Henry. Interview with Ethan Lowens. Personal interview. Philadelphia, July 10, 2013.

91 Ibid.

92 Hazelton, Lynette. "Fattah Offers New Leadership." *The Philadelphia Tribune* 22 Jan. 1982: n. pag. *ProQuest Historical Newspapers*. Web. 16 Jan. 2014

93 Hazelton, Lynette. "Fattah: Not Just Another Candidate." *The Philadelphia Tribune* 23 Feb. 1982: n. pag. *ProQuest Historical Newspapers*. Web. 16 Jan. 2014.

94 Goode, W. Wilson., and Joann Stevens. *In Goode Faith: Philadelphia's First Black Mayor Tells His Story*. Valley Forge, PA: Judson, 1992. Print.

95 Ibid.

96 Ibid.

97 Ibid.

98 Kilbanoff, Hank. "As Debates Go, This One Had Its Unusual Moments." *The Philadelphia Inquirer* 20 Apr. 1983: n. pag. *Access World News.* Web. 6 Feb. 2014.

99 Goode, W. Wilson., and Joann Stevens. *In Goode Faith: Philadelphia's First Black Mayor Tells His Story.* Valley Forge, PA: Judson, 1992. Print.

100 Miller IV, William. Interview with Ethan Lowens. Personal interview. Philadelphia, June 18, 2013.

101 Ibid.

102 Ibid.

103 Goode, W. Wilson., and Joann Stevens. *In Goode Faith: Philadelphia's First Black Mayor Tells His Story.* Valley Forge, PA: Judson, 1992. Print.

104 Ibid.

105 Goode, W. Wilson., and Joann Stevens. *In Goode Faith: Philadelphia's First Black Mayor Tells His Story.* Valley Forge, PA: Judson, 1992. Print.

106 "Center City Philadelphia." *Center City District / Central Philadelphia Development Corporation Of Philadelphia.* N.p., n.d. Web. 13 Feb. 2014.

107 Goode Research Report, May 2013

108 Goode, W. Wilson., and Joann Stevens. *In Goode Faith: Philadelphia's First Black Mayor Tells His Story.* Valley Forge, PA: Judson, 1992. Print.

109 Ibid.

110 Goode Research Report, May 2013

111 Ibid.